D1650485

Family Cycling
TRAILGUIDE

Nick Cotton

Second Edition

© 2000

2

The Routes

Y2K: The Future of Family Cycling

Future generations will look back on the period from 1990 - 2010 as the golden age of the cycle trail, much as the late 18th century saw the creation of our canal network and the middle decades of the 19th century saw the development of the railways. The centrepiece of this cycling renaissance is the National Cycle Network, 10,000 miles of railway paths, canal tow-paths, forestry tracks, riverside paths, traffic-calmed streets and minor lanes that link together all the country's major cities and towns. The Network, with 5000 miles opened in 2000 and the remainder to be built by 2005, has been the brainchild of Sustrans, an engineering charity based in Bristol who have used a £42.5 million National Lottery grant as the impetus to push the £400 million 10 year project (1995 - 2005) to its happy conclusion.

What does this mean for novice cyclists and families with young children and anyone else looking for a safe, easy ride near home or whilst on holiday? Well, what may have been a fairly limited choice of trails a few years ago is growing in variety and quantity year on year. This book pulls together all the traffic-free paths from all over the country into one easy-to-use guide. Many of these are on the National Cycle Network but there are also many that are not: for example most of the waymarked routes on Forestry Commission holdings, the routes around reservoirs and rides in country parks all lie outside the Network.

So, take your pick, look up those popular trails you have heard everyone else talk about when they have come back from holiday or from a good day out or simply look at the map at the back and see which of the trails lie near to home or close to where your relations live or where you have planned to go on holiday. Leap on your bike, feel the wind in your hair, get fit, and do the environment a favour. How many of the trails will you have done a year from now?

As there are ever more paths built each year we apologise if there are some trails which have slipped through the net and we will make every effort to include them in the next edition. Write in your suggestions but much more important - get out and enjoy yourselves!

NICK COTTON

ISBN 0-9533087-4-X

First edition: June 1998. Second edition: July 2000

Printed by Washington Web Limited, Unit 5, Stephenson Road, Stephenson Industrial Estate, Washington, Tyne & Wear NE37 3HR. Tel: 0191 415 7120.

EMAP ACTIVE.
Bretton Court, Bretton, Peterborough PE3 8DZ.
Tel: 01733 264666 Fax: 01733 465990

How to use the Family Cycling Trailguide

Need ideas for a weekend ride? Or a family holiday? Use the list of routes in this book. There are two ways of finding the information you want:

1. You know the name of the trail and you would like to access more information about it.
The routes are all listed together alphabetically. Simply look up the name of the trail and find out details about where to start, the length of the route, refreshments along the way and so on.

2. You want to know what trails there are in your area, or in an area you will be visiting.
Look at the maps at the back of the book, note down the numbers of the routes in that particular area then look up the numbers in the main section of the book.

The routes can be broken down into six main categories:

1. DISMANTLED RAILWAY PATHS.
The beds of dismantled railways make ideal cycling trails: they tend to be flat, broad and stone-based. Sustrans have been converting old railways to recreational use for almost 20 years and many sections are included in their National Cycle Network. We have only included sections of three miles or longer.

2. FORESTRY COMMISSION ROUTES
As with railway paths, forestry tracks offer ideal conditions for recreational cycling: broad stone tracks with the only the occasional Forestry Commission vehicle. There are obviously a lot more hills! Only waymarked routes have been included in the book. This means that all you need to do is arrive at the starting point and follow the waymarked posts.
Forest Enterprise often publish leaflets with details of the routes – these are more useful than the Ordnance Survey map of the area because forest roads change constantly due to logging activities
There are thousands more miles of forestry tracks where you are allowed to ride but where there are no waymarked routes.

3. ROUND RESERVOIR ROUTES
Some water companies have created cycle trails around the perimeter of some of their reservoirs. The quality of the tracks can vary dramatically and most of the routes often involve using short sections of public road.

4. CANAL TOWPATHS
Although there are 2000 miles of canals through the country, only a small fraction of the towpath network is appropriate for cycling. In many cases the towpaths are narrow, overgrown and badly rutted. Even when the surface is in better condition, there are likely to be obstructions in the form of anglers' rods, mooring stakes and low bridges. Canal towpaths are to be savoured slowly – read the Waterways Code at the back of the book.

5. COUNTRY PARKS
Many of these have made some provision for recreational cycling. Some have way-

marked routes, others have a relaxed policy about cycling on stone-based tracks within the parks. The Visitor Centres in the parks are the best source of detailed information.

6. STONE-BASED BRIDLEWAYS/ BYWAYS/LONG DISTANCE TRAILS

Normally suitable only for mountain bikes and better explored in the summer than the winter, there is a vast rights of way network where in some cases you can follow a broad waymarked trail such as the Ridgeway or the South Downs Way for many miles. Only a selection of these have been included, as this book does not have space to list every bridleway in the country!

NB You are not allowed to ride your bike along a footpath.

Sustrans and the National Cycle Network

The most important event to have happened to recreational cycling in Britain in the past few years is the lottery award of £42.5 million given to Sustrans (it stands for Sustainable Transport) to create a 10,000 mile National Cycle Network by the year 2005.

Using a mixture of traffic-free paths and traffic-calmed roads, the network will pass within two miles of twenty million people, linking city to city and town to country, providing routes to serve commuters, shoppers, schoolchildren and recreational cyclists whether out for a day ride or for a trip of a week or more.

At the back of this book you

will find a Sustrans section listing all their long distance routes.

For more information about Sustrans, about how to become a member and how to help create the National Cycle Network, contact:

Sustrans, 35 King Street, Bristol. BS1 4DZ. Tel: 0117 929 0888. www.sustrans.org.uk

Let's hear about your own favourite trails

If we have missed some trails which really ought to make it into the book please write to us. They should be traffic-free and at least three miles long. If they are in forestry they should be waymarked. We would also welcome any details about the state of canal towpaths. If you know of a towpath not mentioned in this book which is a broad, smooth, gravel track with the vegetation kept under good control, write to:

The Family Cycling Trailguide EMAP Active, Apex House, Oundle Road, Peterborough PE2 9NP.

NATIONAL *ycle network*

1. ABBEYFORD WOODS,
north of Okehampton, Devon

A short forest ride in these 380 acres of woodland lying to the north of Okehampton and Dartmoor National Park.

 The route: Waymarked forest route starting from the car park.

Distance: 4 miles.

Category: Woodland trail.

Start + Parking: Car Park in Abbeyford Woods, 2 miles north of Okehampton. Take the B3217 towards Exbourne and Monkokehampton and after 1 mile turn left onto a minor road. Climb steeply and 0.5 mile after entering the woods the car park is on your right.

 Surface + Hills: Forest tracks. Steady climbs.

Roads + Road crossings: A short section of minor road is used.

 Map + Leaflet: OS Landranger Map 191.

Links or other nearby trails: The Tarka Trail starts at Petrockstowe, 12 miles north of Okehampton.

 Refreshments: Lots of choice in Okehampton.

Nearest Railway: Lapford.

2. ABBEYFORD TO CALLANDER IN THE TROSSACHS, north of Glasgow
(See 213 Queen Elizabeth Forest Park)

Aberfoyle is an ideal base for exploring the Trossachs – it is on the National Cycle Network Route 7 from Glasgow to Inverness which runs north and south from Aberfoyle on forestry roads. This ride follows the route between Aberfoyle and Callander.

 The route: Aberfoyle – green waymarked route through Achray Forest – south side of Loch Venachar – Callander.

Distance: 14 miles one way, 28 round trip.

Category: Forest trails.

Start + Parking: Centre of Aberfoyle, on the A81 north of Glasgow or the A84 / A873 west of Stirling. Follow the A821 eastwards for 0.5 mile then turn left signposted 'Dounans Centre'. Bear right uphill through car park and past golf course. At T–junction with forestry track turn left and follow green bike signs.

 Surface + Hills: Forest tracks and stone / gravel path. Steep climb up through Achray Forest.

Roads + Road crossings: Short busy road section at either end of the ride. Longer section on minor no through road west of Callander.

 Map + Leaflet: OS Landranger Map 57. A good map is produced by the Forestry Commission and can be purchased from Aberfoyle Tourist Information Centre. Tel: 01877 382352.

Links or other nearby trails: Several waymarked trails in Queen Elizabeth Forest Park in Loch Ard, Achray and Strathyre Forests.

 Refreshments: Lots of choice in Aberfoyle and Callander. Pub just off the route in Brig o' Turk.

Nearest Railway: Dunblane, east of Callander.

AE (FOREST OF AE) – see 79–80.
Dumfries & Galloway Forestry

---

3. AFAN ARGOED COUNTRYSIDE CENTRE,
east of Port Talbot, South Wales
The Afan Argoed Visitor Centre is an excellent base for many rides in the Afan valley. There are railway paths or waymarked forestry tracks on both sides of the valley heading southwest to Pontrhydyfen and northeast to Blaengwynfi. Spurs lead off to Efail fach and Glyncorrwg.

The route: Pontrhydyfen – Afan Argoed Countryside Centre – Cymer – (optional side trip to Glyncorrwg) – Blaengwynfi.

Distance: 8 miles one way, 16 miles return (plus optional 6 mile round trip from Cymer to Glyncorrwg).

Category: Railway path, forestry trails.

Start + Parking: Afan Argoed Countryside Centre, on the A4107 northeast of Port Talbot (M4 Jct 40).

Surface + Hills: Stone / gravel paths. Gentle climb up the valley towards Blaengwynfi. Steeper climb to cross from one side of the valley to the other.

Roads + Road crossings: Short road section in Cymer.

Cycle Hire: At the Countryside Centre. Tel: 01639 850564.

Map + Leaflet: OS Landranger Map 170. The Forestry Commission produce a fine map which can be purchased from the Countryside Centre. Tel: 01639 850564.

Links or other nearby trails: Neath Canal northeast of Resolven. Ogmore Vale Railway Path from Blackmill to Nant y moel.

Refreshments: At the Countryside Centre. Pubs in Efail fach, Pontrhydyfen, Cymer and Blaengwynfi.

Nearest Railway: Maesteg or Port Talbot.

4. AIRDRIE TO BATHGATE RAILWAY PATH, **east of Glasgow**
One of several long sections of dismantled railway path in the Glasgow area (the others lie to the west of the city). The Airdrie to Bathgate path now forms part of Sustrans Clyde to Forth long distance trail.

The route: Airdrie – Caldercruix – Blackridge – (south of Armadale) – Bathgate.

Distance: 15 miles one way, 30 miles round trip.

Category: Railway path.

Start + Parking:
1. Craigneuk, on the eastern edge of Airdrie just off the A89 Armadale road to the east of the roundabout with the A73.
2. Whiteside, southwest of Bathgate, just off the B7002.
NB This part of Scotland has excellent public transport links where even the trains are bike friendly so do you need to drive?

Surface + Hills: Good quality sealed surface. There is a gentle climb from Bathgate or Airdrie to Hillend Reservoir which is the highest point, in the middle of the ride.

Roads + Road crossings: No major road crossings.

Links or other nearby trails: The new town of Livingston has a fine network of traffic-free cycleways. The Union Canal and Forth & Clyde Canal lie to the north.

Map + Leaflet: OS Landranger Maps 64 + 65. This route plus several others in central Scotland are covered by Sustrans' *Clyde to Forth Cycle Route* map. Available by sending £5.99 to: Sustrans Information Service, PO Box 21, Bristol BS99 2HA, tel: 0117 929 0888.

 Refreshments: Airdrie, Caldercruix, Blackridge and Bathgate.

Nearest Railway: Airdrie or Bathgate.

5. AIRE & CALDER NAVIGATION PATH, southeast from Leeds

Attractive section along this important commercial waterway from the centre of Leeds past Thwaite's Mill Industrial Museum to Woodlesford Metro Train Station.

NB Please read *The Waterways Code – Cycling on the towpath* at the back of this book.

 The route: Leeds city centre southeast to Woodlesford.

Distance: 7 miles one way, 14 miles return.

Category: Canal towpath.

Start + Parking: Woodlesford railway station (just off the A642 to the southeast of Leeds city centre).

 Surface + Hills: Stone and gravel path, no hills.

Roads + Road crossings: None.

Links or other nearby trails: The **Leeds & Liverpool Canal** runs northwest from Leeds city centre.

Map + Leaflet: OS Landranger Map 104.

 Refreshments: At either end of the ride.

Nearest Railway: Leeds or Woodlesford.

6. ALBANWAY – from St Albans to Hatfield, Hertfordshire

Although the instructions to get to the start are complicated, it is well worth exploring this fine wooded railway trail between these two towns. There is a deep cutting at the St Albans end.

 The route: St Albans (Abbey Station) – Hatfield (Galleria Shopping Centre).

Distance: 4.5 miles one way, 9 miles both.

Category: Railway path.

Start + Parking:
1. **St Albans**, near the Abbey Railway Station. Follow the A5183 Radlett Road out of St Albans. At the traffic lights by the Abbey Theatre car park, just after a petrol station on the left but before the Abbey Railway Station, turn left on to Prospect Road. At the T–junction at the end of Prospect Road turn right and park near to the newsagents / stores. To get to the start of the railway path follow the road for 300 yards, cross the railway bridge then turn immediately right and keep bearing right to go back under the bridge and join the railway path.

2. **Hatfield**. The Galleria Shopping Centre surface car park nearest to the Drive–In McDonalds at the back of the cinema complex. From Jct 3 of the A1(M) follow signs for 'Galleria' then for 'A1001 Hertford'. At the roundabout by the Peugeot dealer turn right signposted 'Galleria Parking' and bear left into the surface car park. Park at the far right–hand end near to the Drive–In McDonalds. To get to the start of the trail exit the car park and turn right alongside

the decorative brick wall. Follow this road to its end, staying close to the wall, then climb the ramp / steps and turn right on to the tarmac path. Use the underpass, turn right, cross the bridge then turn left on to the railway path.

 Surface + Hills: Fine gravel path, no hills.

Roads + Road crossings: Several minor roads to cross.

Links or other nearby trails: The **Ayot Greenway**, **Cole Greenway** and **Nicky Line** all lie close by.

 Map + Leaflet: OS Landranger Map 166.

 Refreshments: Lots of choice in St Albans.

Nearest Railway: Abbey Station, St Albans.

7. ALICE HOLT FOREST, southwest of Farnham, Surrey
An easy, well-designed route on the sandy soils south of Farnham, part of the greensand strata that runs east from Alton, between the chalk of the North Downs and the clay of the Weald providing well-drained tracks that are often easier in the winter than the summer!

 The route: Well waymarked circular route starting from the Visitor Centre.

Distance: 4 miles.

Category: Forestry trail.

Start + Parking: At the Visitor Centre, 4 miles southwest of Farnham just off the A325 Farnham – Petersfield road at Bucks Horn Oak (pay and display car park).

 Surface + Hills: Stone/gravel path. Gentle hills.

Roads + Road crossings: None.

Links or other nearby trails: The **Basingstoke Canal** runs from Odiham to Weybridge and pases through Fleet, 5 miles north of Farnham. The **Downs Link** runs from Guildford south to Shoreham.

Cycle Hire: At the Visitor Centre. Tel: 01420 476612. Also at Alice Holt Woodland Park, Bucks Horn Oak, nr Farnham, Surrey, tel: 0777 584 0807.

 Map + Leaflet: OS Landranger Map 186. Further details from: Forest Enterprise, South East Forest England Forest District, Upper Icknield Way, Aston Clinton, Aylesbury HP22 5NF. Tel: 01296 625 825

 Refreshments: At the Visitor Centre (but only basics such as chocolate).

Nearest Railway: Bentley, 2 miles NE.

8. ALTON WATER, south of Ipswich
One of the few reservoirs in East Anglia where it is possible to cycle. There is an offroad circuit and also a quiet lane circuit for the winter months when the going may be muddy on the tracks.

 The route: Round reservoir route starting from the Visitor Centre, near Sutton.

Distance: 8 miles.

Category: Round reservoir route.

Start + Parking: The Visitor Centre, signposted off the B1080, 3 miles west of the A137 Colchester – Ipswich road.

Surface + Hills: A mixture of fine gravel paths and some rougher grass sections. Gently undulating track.

Roads + Road crossings: Short road section south of Tattingstone.

Links or other nearby trails: The **Three Forest Way** lies to the east of Woodbridge.

Cycle Hire: Alton Water Cycle Hire, Holbrook Road, Sutton, Ipswich. Tel: 01473 328873.

 Map + Leaflet: OS Landranger Map 169.

 Refreshments: At the Visitor Centre. Pubs at Tattingstone and Holbrook.

Nearest Railway: Manningtree and Ipswich.

9 – 13. ARGYLL FOREST PARK, Cowal Peninsula, northwest of Glasgow
The park lies on the Cowal Peninsula to the west of the Firth of Clyde and Loch Long and is approached either by ferry from Gourock to Dunoon or the A82 / A83 via Arrochar. There are five waymarked trails.

 9. CAT CRAIG LOOP
Starting point Ardgartan Visitor Centre (A83 west of Arrochar)
Distance 5 miles
Grade Medium
Waymarks Green

 10. ARDGARTAN Peninsula Circuit
Starting point As above or Lochgoilhead
Distance 20 miles
Grade Difficult
Waymarks Red

11. GLENBRANTER SPLASH

Starting point Glenbranter (A815, south of Loch Fyne)
Distance 6 miles
Grade Difficult
Waymarks Red

12. GLENSHELLISH LOOP

Starting point Glenbranter (A815, south of Loch Fyne)
Distance 8 miles
Grade Easy
Waymarks Blue

13. LOCH ECK SHORE

Starting point Glenbranter (A815, south of Loch Fyne)
Distance 9 miles
Grade Easy
Waymarks Green

 Surface + Hills: Forest tracks. Some muddy sections on the Difficult grades. Hills on the Medium and Difficult grades.

Roads + Road crossings: Sections of the longer routes are on quiet public roads.

Links or other nearby trails: Lots more waymarked forest trails in **Queen Elizabeth Forest Park, Aberfoyle.**

 Map + Leaflet: OS Landranger Map 56. Excellent leaflet produced by the Forestry Commission can be purchased from the Visitor Centre or from Forest Enterprise, Cowal Forest District, Kilmun, By Dunoon, Argyll. PA23 8SE. Tel: 01369 84666.

 Refreshments: At the Visitor Centre, Ardgartan. Hotel at Lochgoilhead. Tea rooms at Benmore, south of Glenbranter.

Nearest Railway: Tarbet.

---

14. ASHBY CANAL, north of Coventry

The canal can be followed from Whitestone (to the southeast of Nuneaton) to its terminus near Snarestone (south of Ashby de la Zouch).

NB Please read *The Waterways Code – Cycling on the towpath* at the back of this book.

 The route: Southeast side of Nuneaton (B4114) – Hinckley – Stoke Golding – Congerstone – Shackerstone – Snarestone.

Distance: 20 miles one way, 40 miles both.

Category: Canal towpath.

 Surface + Hills: Some rough and rutted sections. No hills.

Roads + Road crossings: None.

Links or other nearby trails: Ashby Woulds Moira Heritage Trail lies just to the north of the Terminus.

 Map + Leaflet: OS Landranger Maps 128 and 140.

 Refreshments: Pubs in the villages along the way.

Nearest Railway: Hinckley

15. ASHBY WOULDS MOIRA HERITAGE TRAIL, NW of Leicester

Short section of dismantled railway near to the Moira Blast Furnace, one of the best preserved furnaces from the Napoleonic War period.

 The route: Moira – Donisthorpe – Measham.

Distance: 3 miles one way, 6 miles return.

Category: Railway path.

Start + Parking: Moira Furnace car park, off the B5003, 6 miles SE of Burton on Trent.

 Surface + Hills: Stone and gravel path.

Roads + Road crossings: One short stretch on minor road through Donisthorpe.

Links or other nearby trails: The **Derby to Melbourne Path** lies 9 miles to the NE.

 Map + Leaflet: OS Landranger Map 128.

 Refreshments: Pubs in Moira, Donisthorpe, Oakthorpe and Measham.

Nearest Railway: Burton upon Trent.

16. ASHRIDGE ESTATE, northwest of Hemel Hempstead, Hertfordshire

The Ashridge Estate produces a good map showing all the bridleways which criss–cross the beechwoods at this northeast end of the Chilterns.

 The route and distance: There are 9 miles of bridleways in the estate.

Category: Bridleways and roads through Ashridge Estate.

Start + Parking: Visitor Centre, signposted off the B4056 north of Berkhamsted.

 Surface + Hills: Mix of stone-based tracks and rough ones.

Roads + Road crossings: Some sections of quiet lanes.

Links or other nearby trails: The **Grand Union Canal** runs close by. The **Ridgeway / Icknield Way** has some long bridleway sections. There are waymarked forest trails in **Wendover Woods** between Wendover and Tring.

 Map + Leaflet: OS Landranger Map 165. A good map can be purchased from: National Trust, Ashridge Estate Office, Ringshall, Berkhamsted, Hertfordshire. HP4 1LT. Tel: 01442 842488.

 Refreshments: In Aldbury and Little Gaddesden.

Nearest Railway: Tring Station.

17. ASHTON CANAL, from Ashton–under–Lyne to Manchester

One of the few canal towpaths in the northwest where it is possible to cycle. This ride starts in the heart of Manchester and runs east towards the Pennine foothills.

 The route: Manchester city centre east to Ashton-under-Lyne.

Distance: 7 miles one way, 14 miles round trip.

Category: Canal towpath.

Start and parking:
1. Portland Basin, Ashton.
2. Ducie Street Basin, Manchester.

Surface + Hills: Gravel towpath. Steep gradient alongside locks .

Roads + Road crossings: None.

Links or other nearby trails: The **Middlewood Way** runs south from Marple to Macclesfield.

 Map + Leaflet: OS Landranger Map 109.

 Refreshments: Lots of choice in Ashton and Manchester.

Nearest Railway: Ashton from Manchester Victoria and Guide Bridge from Manchester Piccadilly.

18. ASHTON – PILL RIVERSIDE PATH, Bristol

Explore the broad riverside path running beneath the Clifton Suspension Bridge, one of Isambard Kingdom Brunel's finest creations. The path runs for 5 miles along the bottom of the gorge. The tidal rise and fall of the Bristol Channel is one of the highest in the world.

 The route: (Bristol city centre) Cumberland Road – CREATE Centre – riverside path beneath Clifton Suspension Bridge–Ham Green (Pill).

Distance: 5 miles one way, 10 miles round trip.

Category: Riverside path.

Start + Parking:
1. From Bristol city centre. The riverside path starts from opposite house number 78 on Cumberland Road. (There is parking just beyond here on the left hand side of the road, heading away from the centre). To get here from the Arnolfini Art Gallery cross Prince Street Bridge past the Lifeboat Museum. At the roundabout turn right on to the Cumberland Road. 300 yards past the footbridge over the river bear left on to the cobbled path by the metal railings opposite no. 78. Follow past the first large redbrick warehouse, turn left over the grey steel bridge then right on the asphalt path alongside the river.

2. From Leigh Woods. Cross the Suspension Bridge away from Clifton then take the first right on North Road. Follow this for 0.75 mile. Just after the third turning on the left you will see the wooden gates on your right into the wood marking the start of the track through the woods to join the Avon Gorge path. There is parking for a few cars near here.

 Surface + Hills: Tarmac and fine gravel path. Some mud after rain. Steep hill if you start in Leigh Woods.

Roads + Road crossings: None.

Links or other nearby trails: The **Bristol and Bath Railway Path** starts from the other side of the city from Midland Road. The **Kennet & Avon Canal** runs from Bath east towards Hungerford. There is a waymarked trail in the **Forest of Dean.**

 Map + Leaflet: OS Landranger Map 172.

 Refreshments: At the CREATE Centre. Pubs in Pill, 1 mile beyond the end of the path.

Nearest Railway: Temple Meads, Bristol.

19. ASTON HILL WOODS, north of Wendover, Buckinghamshire
A short, very challenging waymarked route on the steep wooded slopes at the northeastern end of the Chilterns. Not really recommended for anything other than very fit families! For an easier ride try the nearby trail in Wendover Woods.

 The route: Waymarked trail from car park.

Distance: 3 miles.

Category: Steep forest trail.

Start + Parking: Follow the A4011 Tring road out of Wendover for 2.5 miles then turn right on a minor road towards St Leonards and Buckland Common. There is a car park on the left after 0.5 mile.

 Surface + Hills: Forest tracks. Steep hills.

Roads + Road crossings: None.

Links or other nearby trails: There is an easier, family route in Wendover Woods**.** The **Grand Union Canal** runs close by (northwest of Tring). The **Ashridge Estate** has a network of bridleways. The **Ridgeway / Icknield Way** has some long bridleway sections.

 Map + Leaflet: OS Landranger Map 165. Leaflet available from Chilterns Forest Office, Upper Icknield Way, Aston Clinton, Aylesbury Bucks. HP22 5NF. Tel: 01296 625825.

 Refreshments: In Wendover.

Nearest Railway: Wendover.

20. AUCKLAND WAY, south of Durham
Attractive tree-lined route with fine views over the Wear valley towards the hills of the North Pennines.

 The route: Bishop Auckland to Spennymoor.

Distance: 4 miles one way, 8 miles return.

Category: Railway path.

Start + Parking: Princess Street, Spennymoor. Exit the roundabout at the top of Spennymoor High Street onto Clyde Terrace ('Whitworth Hall') then turn right into Princess Street. There is also a car park on Whitworth Road.

 Surface + Hills: Stone path, rough in places. Mountain bikes recommended. Gentle gradients.

Roads + Road crossings: Two minor roads to cross. Busier roads from the south end of the trail into Bishop Auckland.

Links or other nearby trails: The **Brandon to Bishop Auckland Walk** starts from the north of Bishop Auckland.

 Map + Leaflet: OS Landranger Map 93. A fine set of laminated route cards covering 7 railway paths in County Durham can be purchased from The Countryside Group, Environment & Technical Services Dept., Durham County Council, County Hall, Durham. DH1 5UQ. Tel: 0191 383 4144.

 Refreshments: Bishop Auckland.

Nearest Railway: Bishop Auckland.

21. AYOT GREENWAY, Wheathampstead, Hertfordshire
A short ride along the course of the old Luton, Dunstable and Welwyn Junction railway with some lovely wooded sections.

 The route: Wheathampstead east to the minor road south of Welwyn.

Distance: 3 miles one way, 6 miles both.

Category: Railway path.

Start + Parking: Free car park on East Street, Wheathampstead (by the Bull pub), just off the B651, 5 miles north of St Albans. From the bridge over the river follow the 'Bridleway to Waterend' signpost.

 Surface + Hills: Stone–based path, one rougher section near the start. No hills.

Roads + Road crossings: None.

Links or other nearby trails: The **Nicky Line**, **Cole Greenway** and **Albanway**.

 Map + Leaflet: OS Landranger Map 166.

 Refreshments: In Wheathampstead (and Welwyn, 1.5 miles beyond the end of the trail on minor roads).

Nearest Railway: Welwyn North or Harpenden.

22. BANGOR – TREGARTH (Lôn Las Ogwen or Lôn Bach), North Wales
One of three dismantled railways in this part of the world (the other two start in Caernarfon) with fine views of the spectacular mountains of Snowdonia.

 The route: Porth Penryn (Bangor) – Maesgeirchen – Glasinfryn – Tregarth.

Distance: 4.5 miles one way, 9 miles both.

Category: Railway path.

Start + Parking: Bangor, just off the A5122 or Tregarth, 4 miles to S on the B4409.

Surface + Hills: Stone and gravel path. Steady climb south from the coast up to Tregarth.

Roads + Road crossings: The B4409 is crossed twice.

Links or other nearby trails: There are 2 trails running N and S from **Caernarfon**.

Map + Leaflet: OS Landranger Map 115. A free leaflet showing the three railway paths in Gwynedd is available from: Planning & Economic Development Department, Gwynedd Council, Caernarfon, Gwynedd. LL55 1SH. Tel: 01286 672255.

Refreshments: Lots of choice in Bangor. Pub in Tregarth.

Nearest Railway: Bangor.

23. BARMOUTH – DOLGELLAU (Mawddach Estuary), mid Wales

One of the most scenic railway paths in the country, running along the spectacular and atmospheric Mawddach Estuary. Thought by many to be more beautiful then the Camel Trail, yet with a fraction of the visitors!

The route: Barmouth Bridge – Penmaenpool – junction of A493 and A470 to the east of Dolgellau.

Distance: 6.5 miles one way, 13 miles both.

Category: Railway path.

Start + Parking: The Harbour in Barmouth. Car parks also on the south side of Barmouth Bridge at Morfa Mawddach Station and at Penmaenpool (on the A493 to the west of Dolgellau).

Surface + Hills: Stone and gravel path. No hills.

Roads + Road crossings: Short section on road at the start in Barmouth.

Links or other nearby trails: Forest trails in **Coed y Brenin** north of Dolgellau. Railway path north from Criccieth to **Caernarfon**.

Cycle Hire: At Penmaenpool.

Map + Leaflet: OS Landranger Map 124.

Refreshments: Lots of choice in Barmouth. Pub at Penmaenpool.

Nearest Railway: Barmouth.

24. BASINGSTOKE CANAL, Hampshire and Surrey.

A top–grade canal towpath passing through some lovely deep wooded cuttings. The trail can be linked via the *Wey Navigation* to the *Thames Towpath*, taking you right into London at Putney Bridge. The Surrey section of the towpath (north and east of Aldershot) is in better condition than the Hampshire section.

NB Please read *The Waterways Code – Cycling on the towpath* at the back of this book

The route: Greywell (5 miles east of Basingstoke) – Fleet – Ash – Woking – Weybridge.

Distance: Anything up to 32 miles one way (64 miles round trip). The best section is the 8 mile stretch between Ash and Brookwood.

Category: Canal towpath.

Start + Parking:
1. Odiham Wharf car park, Odiham.
2. In Fleet, just off the B3013 by the traffic lights at the bridge over the canal.
3. Basingstoke Canal Centre, Mytchett.
4. Brewery Road car park, Woking.

 Surface + Hills: Mainly good quality gravel path. Some rougher sections in the Hampshire section. No hills.

Roads + Road crossings: Several road crossings (whenever the towpath changes sides).

Links or other nearby trails: This ride can be linked via the **Wey Navigation** at Weybridge to the **Thames Towpath** to take you right into London (Putney Bridge).

 Map + Leaflet: OS Landranger Maps 176 + 186. An excellent map of the whole canal can be purchased from: GEOprojects Ltd., 9–10 Southern Court, South Street, Reading RG1 4QS. Tel: 0118 939 3567.

 Refreshments: Lots of choice along the way.

Nearest Railway: Hook is the nearest station to the start in Greywell. There are stations all along the route.

25. BEDGEBURY FOREST,
Hawkhurst, Kent
The only waymarked forestry route in Kent, this one explores the woodlands to the east of **Bewl Reservoir**. *The Bedgebury Pinetum has a magnificent collection of trees and flowering shrubs.*

 The route: Waymarked forest trail starting from near Louisa Lodge at the eastern end of the forest.

Distance: 3 miles.

Category: Forest trail.

Start + Parking: Turn off the A229 Cranbrook – Hawkhurst Road 2 miles to the north of Hawkhurst onto Park Lane, a minor lane to the west of the main road. Park near to Louisa Lodge.

 Surface + Hills: Stone and gravel path. Gently undulating.

Roads + Road crossings: None.

Links or other nearby trails: **Bewl Water** lies just to the west.

 Map + Leaflet: OS Landranger Map . Pack of 4 laminated leaflets available *Parish Pedals* includes an 8 mile circuit of Bedgebury Forest. Details from: Kent High Weald Project 01580 712771.

 Refreshments: At Bedgebury Pinetum.

Nearest Railway: Etchingham, southwest of Hawkhurst.

26. BELLEVER FOREST,
Dartmoor, Devon
This is one of the few waymarked forest routes in the West Country, this one lies high up in the heart of Dartmoor, just off the only road which goes right across the moor.

The route: Waymarked forest route starting from the car park in Bellever.

Distance: 5 miles.

Category: Forest trails.

Start + Parking: The car park in Bellever Forest, 11 miles northeast of Tavistock.
1. (From the east) Take the B3212 south-west from Moretonhampstead towards Tavistock for 10 miles. Shortly after crossing the Dart River at Postbridge take the first left. Follow this lane for 1 mile.

2. (From the west) Take the B3357 east from Tavistock for 7 miles towards Moretonhampstead. Shortly after crossing the River Dart in Two Bridges turn left on the B3212 continuing towards Moretonhampstead. After 3.5 miles take the first turning right.

 Surface + Hills: Forest tracks. Fairly hilly!

Roads + Road crossings: A short section of minor road is used.

Links or other nearby trails: The **Dartmoor (Princetown)** route starts 5 miles to the southwest. The **Plym Valley Trail** lies 12 miles to the southwest (at Goodameavy).

 Map + Leaflet: OS Landranger Map 191. Leaflet can be purchased from Forest Enterprise, Bullers Hill, Kennford, Devon. EX6 7XR. Tel: 01392 832262.

 Refreshments: Pub at Postbridge.

Nearest Railway: None nearby.

BETWS Y COED FOREST – see 121. **Gwydyr Forest**

27. BEWL WATER, Lamberhurst, Kent
The only round reservoir route south of London, Bewl Water offers a magnificent summer ride through woodland and pasture. Be warned that the surface can be rough and rutted and the route should be avoided after prolonged rain.

 The route: The route starts from the back of the brick building housing the cafe, opposite the terrace. The route is waymarked with 'Round Water Route' signs but the way-marking is patchy and it is not sufficient to say 'follow the edge of the lake' as the route veers away from the water's edge on the southern part of the ride. On the tarmac sections, keep an eye out for 'Round Water Route' signs at each junction.

Distance: 12.5 miles.

Category: Round reservoir route.

Start + Parking: The Visitor Centre, Bewl Water, near Lamberhurst, off the A21 between Tunbridge Wells and Hastings. There is a charge to use the car park.

 Surface + Hills: Varied. There are sections of tarmac, good gravel track, grass and some rough and rutted stretches. The route is closed in winter because of the mud. Avoid the trail after prolonged rain. Several short hills.

Roads + Road crossings: There are short sections of lanes but these carry very little traffic and people around here are used to cyclists.

Links or other nearby trails: There is a waymarked route in **Bedgebury Forest**, just to the east of the reservoir. The **Cuckoo Trail** runs from Polegate to Heathfield.

Cycle Hire: Available at the Visitor Centre. Open at weekends May, June and September. Open daily July and August. Tel: 0860 386144.

 Map + Leaflet: OS Landranger Map 188. A map is available at the Visitor Centre.

 Refreshments: At the Visitor Centre or The Bull pub at Three Leg Cross about half way around the circuit.

Nearest Railway: Wadhurst.

28. BIDDULPH VALLEY TRAIL, Congleton, Cheshire

The raised track bed provides fine views across towards the Peak District. The ride passes through woodland and beneath a magnificent viaduct near Congleton.

 The route: Congleton (off the A54 Buxton Road) south to Biddulph.

Distance: 5 miles one way, 10 miles both.

Category: Railway path.

Start + Parking:
1. Congleton. The track / lane to the right of the Brunswick Wharf Depot (owned by Congleton Borough Council) opposite Brook Street Garage and petrol station, 0.5 of a mile out of Congleton on the A54 Buxton Road.

2. Biddulph. Leave the A527 Congleton to Stoke road at the traffic lights at the southern end of Biddulph, turning on to Newpool Road, signposted 'Mow Cop / Brown Lees'. The trail starts beneath the railway bridge after 200 yards.

 Surface + Hills: Stone-based track with some muddy sections in winter and after rain. No hills.

Roads + Road crossings: None.

Links or other nearby trails: The **Rudyard Lake – Leek Trail** lies 4 miles to the east.

 Map + Leaflet: OS Landranger Map 118.

 Refreshments: In Congleton or Biddulph.

Nearest Railway: Congleton.

29. BIRMINGHAM & BLACK COUNTRY CANAL CYCLEWAY

The only section of the immense canal network in and around Birmingham where cycling is encouraged. This situation may change if National Lottery money is directed towards the renovation of all the towpaths in the area.
NB Please read *The Waterways Code – Cycling on the towpath* at the back of this book

 The route: Gas Street Basin, Birmingham – Smethwick – Tipton – Coseley – Broad Street Basin, Wolverhampton.

Distance: 14 miles one way, 28 miles both.

Category: Canal towpath.

Start + Parking: The towpath can be joined at any point along the route described above. Parking in the side streets.

 Surface + Hills: Stone and gravel path. Some muddy sections after rain.

Roads + Road crossings: None.

Links or other nearby trails: The **Kingswinford Railway Walk** runs south from Wolverhampton through Wombourne to Pensnett.

Map + Leaflet: OS Landranger Map 139. Free leaflet available from: British Waterways, Birmingham & Black Country Canals, Bayleys Lane, Tipton, West Midlands, DY4 0PX. Tel: 0121 506 1300.

 Refreshments: All along the way.

Nearest Railway: Wolverhampton, Tipton, Birmingham New Street.

30. BIRMINGHAM & FAZELEY CANAL

The canal was built to link the Birmingham Canal and the Coventry Canal thus opening up a new waterway route to London and the south of England. It was completed in 1789.

NB Please read *The Waterways Code – Cycling on the towpath* at the back of the book

 The route: Minworth (Caters Bridge, at the junction of the A38 and A4097 southeast of Sutton Coldfield) to Fazeley Junction, south of Tamworth.

Distance: 8.5 miles one way, 17 miles both.

Category: Canal towpath

 Surface + Hills: Varying quality including some rough and rutted sections. No hills.

Links or other nearby trails: Sutton Park, Coventry Canal, Birmingham Canal.

 Map + Leaflet: OS Landranger Map 139.

 Refreshments: Pubs in Curdworth and Fazeley.

Nearest Railway: Water Orton or Tamworth.

31. BRAMPTON VALLEY WAY – Northampton to Market Harborough

A good length of railway path including two tunnels where you will need lights. The trail is maintained to a high standard. There are some old steam locomotives and rolling stock at Chapel Brampton.

 The route: Market Harborough – Great Oxendon – Brixworth – Chapel Brampton – A50 north of Northampton.

Distance: 14 miles one way, 28 miles both.

Category: Railway path.

Start + Parking:
1. The Bell Inn, Market Harborough. From the traffic lights in the centre of town follow the A508 Northampton Road for 0.5 mile. The Bell Inn is on your left. The cycle path starts at the back of the pub.

2. From the centre of Northampton follow the A50 towards Leicester for 4 miles. Once out beyond the city limits and into the country take the first right on to Brampton Lane signposted 'Boughton, Moulton, Boughton Cold Store' then immediately turn right again into the car park.

 Surface + Hills: Good quality stone and gravel path. No hills.

Roads + Road crossings: Several minor roads and one busy road to cross – the A508 between Brixworth and Maidwell.

Links or other nearby trails: Rutland Water lies 15 miles to the northeast.

 Map + Leaflet: OS Landranger Maps 141 + 152.

Refreshments: Lots of pubs just off the route (use an OS map to get to the villages).

Nearest Railway: Market Harborough.

32. BRANDON AND BISHOP AUCKLAND WALK, south of Durham
Wonderful views over the Wear Valley on this attractive route which was originally built to carry coal and coke for the industry in Wearside and Tyneside.

The route: Bishop Auckland – Willington – Brandon – B6302, just south of Durham.

Distance: 9.5 miles one way, 19 miles round trip.

Category: Railway path.

Start + Parking: Newton Cap Viaduct car park, just off the A689 Crook Road, on the north side of Bishop Auckland. Or Broompark car park near Durham. From the A167 take the A690 towards Crook then first right on the B6302.

Surface + Hills: Gravel path, stony in places. A few gentle hills.

Roads + Road crossings: Several minor roads to cross and one major one – the A690 near Willington (take care).

Links or other nearby trails: The **Auckland Way** starts to the east of Bishop Auckland. There are links from Broompark picnic site to the **Deerness Valley Walk** and the **Lanchester Valley Walk.**

Map + Leaflet: OS Landranger Maps 88, 92 & 93. A fine set of laminated route cards covering 7 railway paths in County Durham can be purchased from: The Countryside

Group, Environment & Technical Services Dept., Durham County Council, County Hall, Durham. DH1 5UQ. Tel: 0191 383 4144.

Refreshments: Lots of choice in Bishop Auckland. Pubs in Hunwick, Willington and Brancepeth.

Nearest Railway: Bishop Auckland or Durham (2 miles north of the end of the route).

33–35. BRECHFA FOREST, northeast of Carmarthen, West Wales
One of the few areas in the west of Wales where there are traffic-free routes. Three way-marked trails cater for all abilities.

33. EASY ROUTE
Starting point   Aborgorlech
Distance   8 miles
Waymarks   White

34. MEDIUM ROUTE
Starting point   Byrgwm
Distance   5 miles
Waymarks   Green

35. HARD ROUTE
Starting point   Aborgorlech
Distance   15 miles
Waymarks   Red

Start + Parking: Abergorlech car park on the B4310, 17 miles northeast of Camarthen. Also at Byrgwm car park, 3 miles southwest of Abergorlech.

Surface + Hills: Forest trails. Hills.

Roads + Road crossings: None.

Links or other nearby trails: Three trails in **Swansea**. The **Afan Argoed Countryside Centre** lies northeast of Port Talbot.

Map + Leaflet: OS Landranger Map 146. A good leaflet is available from: The Forest District Manager, Forest Enterprise, Llandovery Forest District, Llanfair Road, Llandovery, Dyfed. SA20 0AL. Tel: 01550 720394.

 Refreshments: Excellent pub, the Black Lion, at Abergorlech.

Nearest Railway: Llandeilo, 10 miles southeast of Abergorlech.

36. BRIDGWATER & TAUNTON CANAL, Somerset

Part of the Sustrans **West Country Way**, which runs from Padstow to Bristol, the towpath runs along the western edge of the Somerset Levels and links the two historic Somerset towns of Bridgwater and Taunton.

 The route: Binford Place and Town Bridge, Bridgwater – Huntworth – North Newton – Creech St Michael – Bathpool – Taunton (County Cricket Ground).

Distance: 15 miles one way, 30 miles round trip.

Category: Canal towpath.

Start + Parking:
Market Street car park in Bridgwater. Coal Orchard car park, Taunton.

 Surface + Hills: From stone / gravel path to grassy sections. No hills.

Roads + Road crossings: You will need to spend time on roads to get to the start from the centres of Bridgwater and Taunton.

Links or other nearby trails: The **Quantocks Ridge** is an undulating track for mountain bikes along the top of the ridge.

 Map + Leaflet: OS Landranger Maps 182 + 193. It is also included in Sustrans West Country Way map, which can be purchased from bookshops or from Sustrans, 35 King Street, Bristol. BS1 4DZ. Tel: 0117 929 0888.

 Refreshments: Lots of choice in Taunton and Bridgwater and all along the canal.

Nearest Railway: Taunton or Bridgwater.

37. BRISTOL AND BATH RAILWAY PATH

One of Sustrans first dismantled railway paths, the route now carries over a million visits a year. It runs from the heart of Bristol to the outskirts of Bath, passing old steam trains at Bitton Station.

 The route: Bristol Bridge / Castle Green – Gardiner Haskins – St. Philips Road (off Midland Road, near Old Market) – Fishponds – Staple Hill – Warmley – Bitton – Saltford – Brassmills Trading Estate – Riverside path – Bath.

Distance: 13 miles one way, 26 miles both.

Category: Railway path.

Start + Parking: The path runs from Midland Road, St Philips (near to Gardiner Haskins) in the centre of Bristol to Brassmill Lane Trading Estate on the western edge of Bath. There are signposted links from the centres of both cities. Parking in Bitton steam railway station or at the Bath end on the trading estate road.

Surface + Hills: Tarmac path (one short gravel section). No hills.

Roads + Road crossings: Two road crossings, the busy one via a pelican crossing.

Links or other nearby trails: **Ashton–Pill path** can be picked up from the CREATE centre on the Cumberland Road, Bristol. The **Kennet & Avon Canal towpath** starts in Bath and runs for 50 miles towards Hungerford.

Cycle Hire: Avon Valley Cyclery at the back of Bath Spa Railway Station. Tel: 01225 461880.

 Map + Leaflet: OS Landranger Map 172. Leaflet available from Bristol City Council, 4th Floor, Wilder House, Wilder Street, Bristol. BS2 8BH. Tel: 0117 903 6838

 Refreshments: Pubs at Saltford and Bitton.

Nearest Railway: Bristol Temple Meads or Bath.

BRISTOL TO PILL,
see 18. **ASHTON – PILL**

38. CAERNARFON TO BRYNCIR (LÔN EIFION). North Wales

A good long stretch of dismantled railway from the atmospheric castle at Caernarfon south to Bryncir with wonderful views west out to Caernarfon Bay and east to the foothills of Snowdonia. The path forms part of Sustrans Welsh National Route from Cardiff to Holyhead (Lôn Las Cymru).

 The route: Caernarfon – Llanwnda – Penygroes – Bryncir (A487).

Distance: 12 miles one way, 24 miles both.

Category: Railway path.

Start + Parking: Car park by Caernarfon Castle. From the harbour by the castle follow signs for Lôn Eifion and 'National Cycle Network 8'. After 300 yards bear left onto the dismantled railway.

 Surface + Hills: Stone and gravel path. Steady climb southwards.

Roads + Road crossings: One busy road to cross – the A499 near Llanwnda.

Links or other nearby trails: Lôn Las Menai **(Caernarfon –Y Felinheli)** starts from the north of Caernarfon.

 Map + Leaflet: OS Landranger Maps 115 + 124. A free leaflet showing the railway paths in Gwynedd is available from: Planning & Economic Development Department, Gwynedd Council, Caernarfon, Gwynedd. LL55 1SH. Tel: 01286 672255.

 Refreshments: Lots of choice in Caernarfon. Several pubs along the route.

Nearest Railway: Bangor.

39. CAERNARFON TO Y FELINHELI (LÔN LAS MENAI). North Wales

This 4 mile section of dismantled railway links Caernarfon with the old slate harbour of Port Dinorwig (Y Felinheli). There are views of the Menai Strait and across the water to the island of Anglesey.

 The route: Caernarfon east to Y Felinheli (Port Dinorwig).

Distance: 4 miles one way. 8 miles round trip

Category: Railway path.

Start + Parking: The Victoria Dock, Caernarfon. Follow signs for Lôn Las Menai and National Cycle Route 8. Also in Y Felinheli.

 Surface + Hills: Compacted dust path. No hills.

Roads + Road crossings: Short road section in Y Felinheli along Beach Road and High Street.

Links or other nearby trails: There are two other nearby railway paths – **Caernarfon – Bryncir** (Lôn Las Eifion) and **Bangor – Tregarth** (Lôn Las Ogwen). The two Caernarfon routes form part of Sustrans Welsh National Route from Cardiff to Holyhead. There is also a route called **Lon Peris** which runs on one of the old slate railway trackbeds into the village of Llanberis right at the foot of Snowdon.

 Map + Leaflet: OS Landranger Map 115. A free leaflet showing the railway paths in Gwynedd is available from: Planning & Economic Development Department, Gwynedd Council, Caernarfon, Gwynedd. LL55 1SH. Tel: 01286 672255.

 Refreshments: Lots of choice in Caernarfon and Y Felinheli.

Nearest Railway: Bangor.

40. CALLANDER TO STRATHYRE,
northwest of Stirling
You should enjoy spectacular views of Ben Ledi and Loch Lubnaig along the course of this dismantled railway linking Callander with Strathyre. This forms part of Sustrans Glasgow to Inverness route. The route occasionally leaves the railway bed to join waymarked forestry tracks.

 The route: Callander – Falls of Leny – west side of Loch Lubnaig – Strathyre.

Distance: 10 miles one way, 20 miles return.

Category: Railway path and forest tracks.

Start + Parking: In Callander. The route starts at the western edge of Callander on the A84 Crianlarich road. Shortly after the end of the shops in Callander and just beyond the Coppice Hotel on the right, turn left downhill towards the river by a sign 'Strathyre, Balquidder. Alternative route for cyclists'. Also car parking off the A84 at the Falls of Leny and in Strathyre.

 Surface + Hills: Stone and gravel path. Several short climbs where the route leaves the course of the railway to join forestry tracks. Strathyre is 200 ft higher than Callander.

Roads + Road crossings: Short road section from the centre of Callander to the start of the ride. Short lane section in Strathyre.

Links or other nearby trails: Aberfoyle to Callander along the banks of Loch Venachar. Lots of waymarked routes in Queen Elizabeth Forest Park.

 Map + Leaflet: OS Landranger Map 57.

 Refreshments: Lots of choice in Callander and Strathyre.

Nearest Railway: Dunblane.

CAMBELTOWN (MULL OF KINTYRE) – see 268. West of Scotland Forestry

41. CAMEL TRAIL,
Wadebridge, Cornwall

The most popular recreational ride in the country, the Camel Trail runs from Poley's Bridge and the wooded countryside of the upper Camel Valley down to Wadebridge and alongside the picturesque Camel Estuary as far as Padstow. The route will be very busy in July and August.

 The route: Poley's Bridge – Bodmin – Wadebridge – Padstow.

Distance: Poley's Bridge to Bodmin – 6 miles. Bodmin to Wadebridge – 5 miles. Wadebridge to Padstow – 5 miles. ie up to 16 miles one way, 32 miles both

Category: Railway path.

Start + Parking: Several possible starting points and car parks – Poley's Bridge, Bodmin, Wadebridge and Padstow.

 Surface + Hills: Stone / gravel path. Gentle (200 ft) climb from Wadebridge to Poley's Bridge.

Roads + Road crossings: Take care crossing the busy A389 near to Bodmin. Short section on road through Wadebridge to rejoin the railway path.

Other nearby trails: The Camel Trail forms the start of Sustrans **West Country Way** which runs 250 miles from Padstow to Bristol. There is a waymarked forest trail in **Cardinham Woods**, northeast of Bodmin.

Cycle Hire:
Bridge Bike Hire – 01208 813050.
Bridge Cycle Hire – 01208 814545.
Camel Trail Cycle Hire – 01208 814104.
Brinham Cycle Hire – 01841 532594.

Park & Ride – 01208 814303.
Padstow Cycle Hire – 01841 533533.

 Map + Leaflet: OS Landranger Map 200. Leaflet available from the Camel rail & Wildlife Shop, Eddystone Rd, Wadebridge PL27 7AL. Tel: 01208 812883.

 Refreshments: Lots of choice in Bodmin, Wadebridge and Padstow.

Nearest Railway: Bodmin Parkway Station, 6 miles southeast of the trail.

42 – 44. CANNOCK CHASE,
north of Birmingham

Cannock Chase is the remnant of a vast royal hunting forest (chase). It contains one of the largest Country Parks in the Britain (3600 acres). There are three waymarked cycle routes suitable for families.

The routes and distance:
42. Sherbrook Valley Route 9 miles
43. Pepperslade Route 4.5 miles
44. Lady Hill Route 4 miles. Steep climbs

Category: Forest trail.

Start + Parking: Cannock Chase Visitor Centre, 3 miles north of Cannock, off the A460 Rugeley road.

 Surface + Hills: Stone and gravel paths. Undulating routes with steep climbs on the Lady Hill Route.

Roads + Road crossings: Several crossings of minor roads.

Links or other nearby trails: The **Stafford-Newport Greenway** is a dismantled railway running west from Stafford.

Map + Leaflet: OS Landranger Maps 127 + 128. A leaflet can be purchased from the Visitor Centre (Tel: 01543 871773) or from the County Countryside Officer, Shire Hall, Market Street, Stafford. ST16 2LQ. Tel: 01785 277264.

 Refreshments: At the Visitor Centre.

Nearest Railway: Rugeley.

45. CARDINHAM WOODS, Bodmin, Cornwall
650 acres of woodland with car park, cafe and cycle hire during the summer and other Bank Holidays. Nearly 70 years of careful management has created a varied and attractive forest. Each age of tree is home to a different range of wildlife. Look out for ravens and buzzards soaring above the forest. Catch the occasional glimpse of grey squirrels, rabbits or foxes. Red and Roe deer are here but melt away into the forest at the first hint of danger.

Distance: 4.5 miles.

Category: Forest trails.

Start + Parking: Cardinham Woods lie 3 miles east of Bodmin. From Bodmin take the Plymouth road (A38) for 2 miles. 400 yds beyond the roundabout turn left signposted 'Cardinham, Fletchersbridge'. After 0.5 mile, just after a sharp bend, turn left and enter the forest.

 Surface + Hills: Stone / gravel path. Gentle gradients.

Roads + Road crossings: None.

Links or other nearby trails: The Camel Trail starts west of Bodmin.

Cycle Hire: Glynn Valley Cycle Hire in Cardinham Woods. Tel: 01208 74244.

 Map + Leaflet: OS Landranger Map 200. For further information contact Forest Enterprise, Peninsula Forest District, Bullers Hill, Kennford, Exeter, Devon. EX6 7XR. Tel 01392 832262.

 Refreshments: Teas at Callywith Cottage, adjacent to the car park at the start.

Nearest Railway: Bodmin.

CARRICK FOREST – see **81. Dumfries & Galloway Forestry**

46. CARSINGTON WATER, northeast of Ashbourne, Peak District
The reservoir was opened in 1992 and immediately became a focus for many leisure activities including cycling, canoeing and sailing.

 The route: Circular route starting from the Visitor Centre.

Distance: 8 miles.

Category: Round reservoir route.

Start + Parking: The Visitor Centre, Carsington Water. Turn off the B5035 Wirksworth – Ashbourne road at the Knockerdown pub.

Surface + Hills: Tarmac. Gravel path. Some rougher surfaces. Several steep sections.

Roads + Road crossings: Almost a quarter of the route is on public roads. The B5035 needs to be crossed at one point.

Links or other nearby trails: The **High Peak & Tissington** and **Manifold Trails**.

Cycle Hire: Carsington Water Cycle Hire, Carsington Water, Ashbourne, Derbyshire. Tel: 01629 540478.

Map + Leaflet: OS Landranger Map 119. Leaflet available from the Visitor Centre.

 Refreshments: At the Visitor Centre. Pub at Carsington village.

Nearest Railway: Belper or Cromford.

47. CASTLE EDEN WALKWAY, northwest of Middlesbrough

A dismantled railway path that has been ear-marked for inclusion into the National Cycle Network. It is at present a fairly narrow path also popular with walkers so please show consideration to other trail users.

 The route: Thorpe Thewles (on the A177 NW of Stockton on Tees) – Hurworth Burn Reservoir (W of the A19, W of Hartlepool).

Distance: 7 miles one way, 14 miles both.

Category: Railway path.

Start + Parking: Car park just off the A689 to the northwest of Billingham.

 Surface + Hills: Stone and gravel path. No hills.

Links or other nearby trails: Hart to Haswell Trail.

 Map + Leaflet: OS Landranger Map 93.

 Refreshments: At the Castle Eden Walkway Country Park Visitor Centre. Pub at Thorpe Thewles.

Nearest Railway: Billingham or Stockton on Tees.

48. CASTLEMAN TRAIL, Wimborne Minster, Dorset

Woodland railway path between Ringwood and Poole on the course of the old Dorchester – Southampton railway. The route is broken into two sections as parts of the railway bed between West Moors and Wimborne Minster have been lost to development.

 The route:
1. Moors Valley Country Park (Ashley Heath, west of Ringwood) – West Moors.
2. Merley (south of Wimborne Minster) – Upton Country Park.

Distance:
1. West Moors to Ashley Heath – 4.5 miles one way, 9 miles round trip.
2. Wimborne Minster to Upton Country Park. 4 miles one way, 8 miles round trip.

Category: Railway path.

Start + Parking:
1. Moors Valley Country Park, off the minor road leading west from the A338 / A31 roundabout to the west of Ringwood.

2. Willet Arms pub, Merley, just south of Wimborne Minster. This lies just off the more southerly of the two roundabouts near the junction of the A31 and A349. If you wish to use the Willet Arms pub car park you must ask permission. You can also start at Upton Country Park, off the A35 just east of Upton.

 Surface + Hills: Gravel path. No hills.

Roads + Road crossings: Busy roads to cross at the southern end to gain access to Upton Country Park.

Links or other nearby trails: Lots of trails in the **New Forest**.

Map + Leaflet: OS Landranger Map 195.

 Refreshments: Tea rooms in the Visitor Centres at Moors Valley Country Park and Upton Country Park.

Nearest Railway: Upton.

49. CENTURION WAY, Chichester

 A short railway path starting from the historic city of Chichester. The name was suggested by a local schoolboy and is based on the fact that the trail crosses the course of a Roman road. There are sculptures along the way.

 The route: Westgate, west Chichester (north of the A27 and west of the college) – Mid Lavant (on the A286 north of Chichester).

Distance: 2.5 miles one way, 5 miles return.

Category: Railway path.

Start + Parking: Westgate, on the west side of Chichester or Warble Heath Close in Mid Lavant, just off the A286 to the north of Chichester.

 Surface + Hills: Fine gravel path, no hills.

Roads + Road crossings: None.

Links or other nearby trails: The South Downs Way is a long distance bridleway between Winchester and Eastbourne.

 Map + Leaflet: OS Landranger Map 197. Leaflet available from: Local Transport Planning Section, West Sussex County Council, Chichester, West Sussex, PO19 1RH. Tel: 01243 777353.

 Refreshments: Lots of choice in Chichester. Pub in Mid Lavant.

Nearest Railway: Chichester or Fishbourne.

 ## 50. CHESHIRE LINES PATH, north of Liverpool

Cycle from the outskirts of Liverpool to the coast south of Southport, following the old Cheshire Lines railway across the West Lancashire Moss.

 The route: Maghull (west of M58, Jct 1) to Ainsdale (south of Southport).

Distance: 10 miles one way, 20 miles both.

Category: Railway path.

Start + Parking:
1. Maghull, off the A59 to the north of the M57, Jct 7. The railway path starts on a sharp right hand bend on the minor road which links the A5147 with the B5195.
2. The railway station, Ainsdale, west of the A565 between Formby and Southport. Follow Easdale Drive and Kendal Way to the start of the railway path.

 Surface + Hills: Tarmac, stone / gravel path. One rough section near Ainsdale. No hills.

Roads + Road crossings: One busy crossing of the A565 in Ainsdale.

Links or other nearby trails: Liverpool Loop Line.

 Map + Leaflet: OS Landranger Map 108. Leaflet available from Sustrans, St Pauls Centre, Hightown, Crewe. CW1 3RY 01270 211030.

 Refreshments: Lots of choice in Maghull and Ainsdale.

Nearest Railway: Maghull or Ainsdale.

51. CHURNET VALLEY TRAIL, west of Ashbourne, Peak District

A railway path through woodland at the southwest edge of the Peak District, running close to Alton Towers. Keep an eye out for the dramatic Gothic-style castle in Alton village to the south of the trail.

 The route: Oakamoor (east of Stoke on Trent) – Alton Towers – Denstone.

Distance: 4 miles one way, 8 miles both.

Category: Railway path.

Start + Parking:
1. The car park in Oakamoor is just off the B5417 at the bottom of the hill just to the west of the bridge over the River Churnet, by the The Cricketers Arms pub. Go past a second pub (the Admiral Jervis) to the end of the second car park and fork left to get to the start of the trail.

2. The Village Hall car park, on the B5032 in Denstone, 5 miles north of Uttoxeter. From the car park, go past the petrol station and turn left just before the telephone box on to the Churnet Railway Trail.

 Surface + Hills: Stone-based track. One or two muddy sections after rain. No hills.

Roads + Road crossings: None.

Links or other nearby trails: The Tissington Trail starts in Ashbourne, 8 miles to the northwest of Denstone. The Manifold Trail starts at Waterhouses, 6 miles northeast of Oakamoor.

 Map + Leaflet: OS Landranger Map 119 or 128.

 Refreshments: The Tavern pub, Denstone. The Admiral Jervis and Cricketers Arms pubs, Oakamoor.

Nearest Railway: Uttoxeter.

CLATTERINGSHAWS FOREST – see **82 – 85. Dumfries & Galloway Forestry**

52. CLIPSTONE FOREST, northeast of Mansfield

A well-signposted trail through this large tract of forestry land. The tracks are wide and well-maintained so this is a good ride for cycling in a group. There is also a much tougher mountain bike trail adjoining the family route if you want a harder challenge.

 The route: Waymarked trail in the forest.

Distance: 6 miles.

Category: Forest trail.

Start + Parking: Sherwood Pines car park, off the B6030, 5 miles northeast of Mansfield.

 Surface + Hills: Forestry tracks/ Undulating landscape.

Roads + Road crossings: None.

Links or other nearby trails: The Southwell Trail, which runs from

---

Southwell to Bilsthorpe, lies 5 miles to the southeast. **Clumber Park** lies 6 miles to the north.

Cycle Hire: Sherwood Pines Cycles. Tel: 01623 822855.

 Map + Leaflet: OS Landranger Map 120. Forest Enterprise also produce a leaflet which is available at the Visitor Centre.

 Refreshments: Cafe at the Visitor Centre.

Nearest Railway: Fiskerton Station, south-east of Southwell.

53. CLUMBER PARK,
southeast of Worksop
Wonderful, cycle-friendly park with miles of tracks and quiet roads to explore at your leisure. It is strongly recommended that you buy a map from the Visitor Centre or Cycle Hire Centre to find your way around.

 The route and distance: There are many miles of fine tracks and quiet estate roads around Clumber Park, through woodland and alongside the lake. The National Trust has waymarked two cycle routes, one of about 5 miles (green waymarkers) and the other of about 13 miles (orange waymarkers). Both start from the cycle hire shop by the car park.

Category: Estate roads and paths.

Start + Parking: Clumber Park lies SE of Worksop (east of M1 Jct 30). There are 5 entrances to the park – off the A57 from the north, off the B6034 to the west and off the A614 to the east. The main car park is near the chapel, restaurant and shops.

 Surface + Hills: Tarmac or good stone and gravel paths. Gentle hills.

Roads + Road crossings: There is some light traffic on the estate roads. The park is busier in high season.

Links or other nearby trails: There is a waymarked trail in **Clipstone Forest**, 6 miles to the south.

 Map + Leaflet: OS Landranger Map 120. Much better is the map produced by the park which can be purchased from The Clocktower Shop, Clumber Park, Worksop, Notts S80 3BE. Tel: 01909 474468 or the Cycle Hire Centre at Duke's Garage, tel: 01909 476592.

 Refreshments: Clumber Restaurant, in the park.

Nearest Railway: Worksop.

54 – 56. COED Y BRENIN FOREST,
north of Dolgellau, mid–Wales
A large Forestry Commission holding in North Wales which has adopted a very positive attitude to recreational cycling with three waymarked trails. Only the Fun Route is suitable for novices or young children.

 Route, distance, grade and waymarking:

54. Fun Route   *Easy*
7 miles   Yellow waymarks
55. Sport Route   *Moderate*
14 miles   Blue waymarks
56. Expert Route   *Strenuous*
22 miles   Red waymarks

Start + Parking: Visitor Centre, off the A470, 9 miles north of Dolgellau.

Surface + Hills: Forest tracks. The Expert and Sport routes contain many technical sections and are **not** for novices! This is a hilly area!

Roads + Road crossings: The A470 is crossed twice on the Expert and Sport Routes.

Links or other nearby trails: The **Barmouth – Dolgellau Trail** lies 9 miles south of the Visitor Centre.

 Map + Leaflet: OS Landranger Map 124. Forest Enterprise leaflet available from the Visitor Centre at Coed y Brenin.

Cycle Hire: At the Visitor Centre. Tel: 01341 440666.

 Refreshments: At the Visitor Centre.

Nearest Railway: Barmouth.

57. COLE GREEN WAY, west of Hertford

The most rural of the four dismantled railways in Hertfordshire, passing through attractive woodland between the Rivers Lee and Mimram.

The route: Welwyn Garden City (southeast edge/off the B195) – Cole Green – Hertford (Hertford FC ground).

Distance: 4.5 miles one way, 9 miles both

Category: Railway path.

Start + Parking:
1. On the southeast edge of Welwyn Garden City. Follow the B195 towards Cole Green and Letty Green. At the start of the countryside at the edge of Welwyn Garden City turn right off the B195 signposted 'QE2

Hospital'. Park on either Holwell Hyde Lane or Holwell Hyde.

2. The Cole Greenway car park near the Cowper Arms pub in Cole Green. Turn off the A414 following signs for 'Cole Green / Birch Green' then for 'Letty Green'. The car park is just beyond the Cowper Arms pub on the left.

3. Hertford Town FC Ground. Take the A414 out of Hertford towards Hatfield. Just after the Gates Ford garage turn left on to West Street signposted 'Hertford Town FC'. About 200 yards after the end of the houses, on a left hand bend, turn right by a bike sign down a tarmac lane leading to the car park.

 Surface + Hills: Fine gravel path, no hills.

Roads + Road crossings: One minor lane to cross.

Links or other nearby trails: The **Ayot Greenway, Albanway** and **Nicky Line** are all nearby.

 Map + Leaflet: OS Landranger Map 166.

 Refreshments: Lots of choice in Hertford. Cowper Arms pub at Cole Green.

Nearest Railway: Hertford.

58. CONSETT AND SUNDERLAND RAILWAY PATH, NE of England

The trail runs along one of Britain's oldest railways, built in 1834. When the track was lifted in 1985, Sustrans converted the path to recreational use and have since decorated the trail with many environmental sculptures. The trail forms part of the C2C.

The route: Consett – Leadgate – Annfield Plain – Stanley – Chester-le-Street – Washington – Pallion – Sunderland (near the bus station).

Distance: 22 miles one way, 44 miles both.

Category: Railway path.

Start + Parking: Hownes Gill car park (off the A692, south of Consett). Also at Consett, Annfield Plain, Stanley, Beamish, Chester-le-Street and James Steel Park, Washington.

 Surface + Hills: Fine gravel and tarmac path. Fairly flat with the exception of the crossing of the River Wear at Washington.

Roads + Road crossings: Several minor roads to cross. Short road sections near Washington and in Pallion, Sunderland.

Links or other nearby trails: At Hownes Gill Viaduct the trail links to the **Waskerley Way, Lanchester Valley Walk** and the **Derwent Walk.**

Cycle Hire: Darke Cycles, 113 High Street West, Sunderland. Tel: 0191 510 8155.

 Map + Leaflet: OS Landranger Map 88. Also covered by Sustrans C2C map.

 Refreshments: The Shepherd and Shepherdess pub at Beamish village or the coffee shop in the Beamish Museum entrance hall.

Nearest Railway: Chester-le-Street, Sunderland.

59. COTSWOLD WATER PARK,
south of Cirencester, Gloucestershire
The well-signposted route takes you among

some of the many lakes formed by gravel extraction and along the course of a dismantled railway. Amongst the other curiosities you may see, keep an eye out for a street in South Cerney called 'Bow Wow'!

 The route: Keynes Country Park – Hailstone Hill – South Cerney – car park on B4696

Distance: 9 miles.

Category: Railway path, bridleways and minor roads.

Start + Parking: Keynes Country Park, or car park on the B4696 south of South Cerney, 4 miles south of Cirencester. From the car park follow signs for 'Bridlepath Circuit. South Cerney, Cricklade'.

 Surface + Hills: Variety – tarmac, bridlepaths, railway path. Mountain bikes recommended. No hills.

Roads + Road crossings: About 1/3 of the route is on Cotswold lanes and streets through South Cerney.

Links or other nearby trails: The **Stonehouse – Nailsworth Trail** and the **River Ray Parkway** lie nearby.

Cycle Hire: Cerney Cycle Hire, Cotswold Hoburne Holiday Centre, Broadway Lane, South Cerney, Cirencester, Glos. Tel : 01285 860216. Go By Cycle, Keynes Country Park. Shorncote, Cirencester, GL7 4DE, tel: 07970 419208.

Map + Leaflet: OS Landranger Map 163. *Cycle Routes in the Cotswold Water Park* is a leaflet describing two cycle routes in the Cotswold Water Park (this one and a purely road route). Send SAE to Rangers Office, Keynes Country Park, Shorncote, Cirencester, Glos. GL7 6DF.

Refreshments: In South Cerney and Ashton Keynes.

Nearest Railway: Kemble.

60. COWES TO NEWPORT CYCLEWAY, Isle of Wight

One of two fine railway paths on the island, which also boasts some fabulous bridleways, particularly the Tennyson Trail in the SW.

 The route: Cowes (Cowes Hotel, Arctic Rd, on SW edge of town) – River Medina – Newport (industrial park on the N edge of town).

Distance: 4 miles one way, 8 miles return.

Category: Railway path.

 Surface + Hills: Mainly tarmac. No hills

Roads + Road crossings: No busy roads to cross. You will need to use fairly busy roads to get to the centre of Newport and Cowes from the start / finish of the cyclepath.

Links or other nearby trails: The **Yarmouth to Freshwater Trail** is at the western end of the island. The chalk ridge of Tennyson Trail from Freshwater to Carisbrooke (Newport) is a superb, challenging ridge ride in the summer months.

Cycle Hire: Offshore Sports, Shooters Hill, Cowes. Tel: 01983 291914.

 Map + Leaflet: OS Landranger Map 196.

 Refreshments: Plenty of choice in Cowes and Newport.

61– 64. CRAIK FOREST, southwest of Hawick, Scottish Borders

10,000 acre forest rising to almost 1500 feet on the boundary of Dumfries & Galloway and the Scottish Borders with four way-marked forest trails.

 Routes, distance, grade and waymarking

61. Easy Route   4 miles
Blue waymarks
62. Intermediate Route   7 miles
Green waymarks
63. Intermediate Route   9 miles
Purple waymarks
64. Demanding Route   8 miles
Red waymarks

Start + Parking: The hamlet of Craik, at the end of the minor road that leads southwest from the B711 Hawick – Ettrick road, 6 miles west of Hawick

 Surface + Hills: Forest tracks. Lots of hills.

Roads + Road crossings: None.

Links or other nearby trails: There are plenty more forest trails in Southern Scotland: see **Tweed Valley Forestry** and **Dumfries & Galloway Forestry**

 Map + Leaflet: OS Landranger Map 79. Forest Enterprise map available from Forest District Manager, Weavers Court, Forest Mill, Selkirk TD7 5NY. Tel: 01750 721120.

 Refreshments: None.

Nearest Railway: Lockerbie.

CRIANLARICH – see 276. West of Scotland Forestry

65. CUCKOO TRAIL,
Hailsham, Sussex
Together with the **Downs Link** and the **Meon Valley Trail,** the Cuckoo Trail is one of the longest railway paths in the southeast of England. The line gained its name because of a Sussex tradition that the first cuckoo of spring was released each year at Heathfield Fair.

The route: Polegate (north of Eastbourne) – Hailsham – Horam – Heathfield.

Distance: 11 miles one way, 22 miles both.

Category: Railway path.

Start + Parking: Heathfield, Hailsham, Horam or Polegate. The car parks are all close to the trail.

Surface + Hills: Tarmac and fine gravel path. Gentle 300 ft climb from Polegate to Heathfield, so it is best to start at the south and climb the hill when you are fresh.

Roads + Road crossings: Several minor roads to cross. The busiest road (B2104) south of Hailsham has a pelican crossing. The route through Hailsham uses short sections of road.

Links or other nearby trails: Friston Forest and Seven Sisters Country Park lie 5 miles to the southeast of Polegate. **The South Downs Way** is a long distance bridleway from Winchester to Eastbourne (100 miles long). The Cuckoo Trail will form part of the Dover–Eastbourne–London leg of the National Cycle Network.

Cycle Hire: Cuckmere Cycle Co. at Horam. Tel: 01435 813000; Cycle Revival, Hailsham Road, Heathfield. Tel: 01435 866118.

Map + Leaflet: OS Landranger Map 199. Leaflet available from Boship Tourist Information Centre, Lower Dicker, Hailsham, East Sussex. BN27 4DT. Tel: 01323 442667.

Refreshments: Lots of choice in each of the towns through which the trail passes.

Nearest Railway: Polegate, less than half a mile from the start of the route.

66 – 69. CWM DARRAN COUNTRY PARK, southeast of Merthyr Tydfil, South Wales
Peaceful country park tucked away from it all in the Darran Valley, 6 miles southeast of Merthyr Tydfil. Displays show the history of the park's development from mining valley to award winning country park. There is a dismantled railway path down to Bargoed and 3 other waymarked mountain bike routes in the park.

The route: Cwm Darran Country Park – north end of Bargoed (in the Rhymney Valley). Plus 3 way-marked mountain bike routes.

Distance:
66. Railway path – 4 miles one way, 8 miles round trip.

Mountain bike routes:
67. Moderate Route 1.7 miles
Green waymarks
68. Intermediate Route 3 miles
Orange waymarks
69. Challenging Route 5.5 miles
Red waymarks

Category: Railway path and waymarked forestry trails.

Start + Parking: Cwm Darran Country Park, on the minor road between the A469 to the north of Bargoed and the A465 to the east of Merthyr Tydfil.

 Surface + Hills: Fine gravel on the railway path. Gentle descent over 4 miles to Bargoed. Rougher surfaces and several steep climbs on the mountain bike routes.

Roads + Road crossings: One minor road to cross in Deri.

Links or other nearby trails: The **Taff Trail** runs from Cardiff to Brecon via Pontypridd and Merthyr Tydfil. There is a dismantled railway in **Sirhowy Valley Country Park** to the west of Risca and Cross Keys. The **Rhondda Community Routes** are waymarked forestry trails in the woodland to the west of Treorchy.

 Map + Leaflet: OS Landranger Map 171. A leaflet is produced by Caerphilly County Borough Council showing the mountain bike trails in Parc Cwm Darran. Tel: 01443 864312.

 Refreshments: At the Visitor Centre. Pub in Deri and several pubs in Bargoed.

Nearest Railway: Bargoed.

DALBEATTIE – see 86 – 87. Dumfries & Galloway Forestry

70. DALBY FOREST, northeast of Pickering, North York Moors
The North Riding Forest Park is made up of 27,000 hectares of woodland, including Dalby, Langdale and Sneaton Forests. There is at present

one waymarked trail but more are planned, starting from the Low Dalby Visitor Centre, 3 miles northeast of Pickering.

Distance: 12 miles.

Category: Forest trails.

Start + Parking: Low Dalby Visitor Centre, just north of Thornton–le–Dale (on the A170 just east of Pickering towards Scarborough). There is a charge to use the toll road. There are also car parks at Bickley Forest Gardens in Langdale Forest and May Beck and Falling Foss in Sneaton Forest.

 Surface + Hills: Forest roads. Lots of hills. Mountain bikes recommended.

Roads + Road crossings: The route uses part of the Forest Drive which can get busy in the summer holidays.

Links or other nearby trails: The **Scarborough to Whitby Railway Path** lies 12 miles to the east. **Guisborough Forest** is 25 miles to the northwest.

Cycle Hire:
Dalby Visitor Centre. Tel: 01751 460295. Wardill Bros, Thornton-le-Dale. Tel: 01751 474335.

 Map + Leaflet: OS Landranger Map 94 & 101. A map is available from the Visitor Centre. Tel: 01751 460295.

 Refreshments: Low Dalby Visitor Centre.

Nearest Railway: Scarborough.

71. DALKEITH – PENICUIK, south of Edinburgh
The longest of the dismantled railways close to Edinburgh and the most scenic, passing through many beautiful wooded cuttings.

The route: Eskbank (southwest edge of Dalkeith) – Bonnyrigg and Lasswade – (south of Roslin) – Penicuik.

Distance: 8 miles one way, 16 miles both.

Category: Railway path.

Start + Parking:
1. The Eskbank Post Office, Lasswade Road, on the southwest edge of Dalkeith (just off the 6 road roundabout at the junction of the A768 and A6094)
2. The octagonal church at the junction of the A701 and B6372 on the southeast edge of Penicuik.

Surface + Hills: Stone and gravel path. Steady climb from Dalkeith to Penicuik.

Roads + Road crossings: The busy A704 needs to be crossed in Lasswade. The B7003 is crossed near Rosewell. Short sections of minor lanes are used.

Links or other nearby trails: The Pencaitland Railway Walk starts 3 miles northeast of Dalkeith. The Water of Leith runs southwest from Edinburgh through Balerno.

Map + Leaflet: OS Landranger Map 66. An excellent map of the whole Midlothian area can be purchased from SPOKES, The Lothian Cycle Campaign, St Martin's Church, 232 Dalry Road, Edinburgh, EH1 2JG. Tel: 0131 313 2114.

Refreshments: Lots of choice in Dalkeith and Penicuik.

Nearest Railway: Musselburgh.

72. DEERNESS VALLEY WALK, west of Durham

The landscape of this area was shaped by the coalmining industry in the 19th century although little sign is left nowadays as the area has greened over. The trail runs west from Durham, crossing and re-crossing the River Deerness.

The route: Broompark car park (B6302, west of Durham) – Esh Winning – Waterhouses – B6299 (Stanley Crook).

Distance: 8 miles one way, 16 miles both.

Category: Railway path.

Start + Parking: Broompark picnic site, south of Durham. From the A617 take the A690 towards Crook then first right on the B6302. The car park is signposted to the left.

Surface + Hills: Fine gravel path, moderate gradients. Steep climb at the end of the Stanley Crook end of the ride.

Roads + Road crossings: Several minor roads to cross. Busy roads into Durham or Crook from either end of the trail.

Links or other nearby trails: From Broompark car park to Lanchester Valley Walk and Brandon to Bishop Auckland Walk.

Map + Leaflet: OS Landranger Maps 88 + 92. A fine set of laminated route cards covering 7 railway paths in County Durham can be purchased from The Countryside Group, Environment & Technical Services Dept., Durham County Council, County Hall, Durham. DH1 5UQ. Tel: 0191 383 4144.

Refreshments: Pubs and cafe in Esh Winning and Crook. Pub at Hamilton Row (west of Waterhouses).

Nearest Railway: Durham Station is 2 miles from Broompark car park.

73. DELAMERE FOREST,
east of Chester
The only waymarked forest trail in this part of the world, the woodland is situated conveniently close to Delamere railway station. There are many miles of forest roads to explore in addition to the waymarked trail.

Distance: 5 miles.

Category: Forestry trails.

Start + Parking: Forestry Commission Discovery Centre, Linmere, Delamere, just off the B5152, 6 miles south of M56, Jct 12.

 Surface + Hills: Forest tracks.

Roads + Road crossings: A minor road needs to be crossed twice.

Links or other nearby trails: The **Whitegate Way** starts 3 miles to the east.

Cycle Hire: Groundwork Trust, Discovery Centre, Linmere, Delamere, Cheshire. Tel 01606 40555.

 Map + Leaflet: OS Landranger Map . Delamere Forest Guide Map can be purchased from Forest Enterprise, Linmere, Delamere, Cheshire. Tel 01606 882167.

 Refreshments: At the Visitor Centre.

Nearest Railway: Delamere.

74. DERBY – ELVASTON CASTLE COUNTRY PARK
A fine escape from the heart of Derby via a top quality track alongside the River Derwent to the Elvaston Castle Country Park where there is the option of a circuit around the park.

 The route: The Council House, in the centre of Derby – Bass's Recreation Ground – Derwent riverside path – Elvaston Castle Country Park.

Distance: 4.5 miles one way, 9 miles both.

Category: Riverside path.

Start + Parking:
1. The Council Offices, Derby City Centre, on the south side of the bridge over the River Derwent.

2. If arriving by car it would be better to start at Elvaston Castle Country Park. Turn off the A6005 Derby – Long Eaton road in Borrowash onto the B5010 towards Elvaston. The entrance to the park is 1.5 miles along on the right. (The B5010 can also be approached from the A6 Derby – Loughborough Road). From the castle head north to join the riverside path.

 Surface + Hills: Fine gravel path. No hills.

Roads + Road crossings: None.

Links or other nearby trails: The trail links with the **Derby – Melbourne Trail.** The **Nutbrook Trail** is also nearby.

Cycle Hire:
At Elvaston Castle Tel: 0115 939 8858.

 Map + Leaflet: OS Landranger Maps 128 + 129. An excellent leaflet called *Recreational Routes in and around Derby* is available from

---

Derby City Council, Planning and Technical Services Dept, Roman House, Friar Gate, Derby. DE1 1XB. Tel: 01332 255021.

 Refreshments: Tea rooms at Elvaston Castle.

Nearest Railway: Derby.

75. DERBY TO MELBOURNE

*Derby is well provided with recreational cycle routes – this one follows the same course as the **Derby-Elvaston Park** route at the start before turning south away from the River Derwent and using the course of a former canal to reach the village of Melbourne, some 8 miles south of the city centre, and then 4 miles on to Worthington on a former railway track.*

 The route: Derby city centre (Council House) – River Derwent waterside path – Crewton – Allenton – Chellaston – Swarkestone – King's Newton (northeast of Melbourne) – Tonge – Worthington.

Distance: 12 miles one way, 24 miles both.

Category: Canal towpath/rail path

Start + Parking: The ride starts from the heart of Derby, by the Council House. If arriving by car start at the Alvaston Recreation Ground on the A6, 2 miles from Derby city centre (opposite the Wickes DIY centre). This start point can be used for this route and the previous one – in fact, the car park is close to the junction where the two trails divide.

 Surface + Hills: Stone and gravel path. No hills.

Roads + Road crossings: Several road crossings, some use pelican crossings. The extension of the route from Melbourne to Worthington uses a 3/4 mile length of the Swarkestone to Weston on Trent minor road which can be quite busy. However, a section of the Trent and Mersey canal towpath is being improved so this stretch of road can be eliminated.

Links or other nearby trails:
The **Derby – Elvaston Castle Country Park Route** is close by.

 Map + Leaflet: OS Landranger Map 128. An excellent leaflet called *Recreational Routes in and around Derby* is available from Derby City Council, Planning and Technical Services Dept, Roman House, Friar Gate, Derby. DE1 1XB. Tel: 01332 255021.

 Refreshments: Lots of choice in Derby and Melbourne.

Nearest Railway: Derby.

DERWENT VALLEY RESERVOIRS (PEAK DISTRICT) –see 260. Upper Derwent Valley Reservoirs

76. DERWENT VALLEY WALK, southwest of Newcastle upon Tyne

Running along the course of the old Derwent Valley Railway, the trail follows the River Derwent, a tributary of the Tyne, passing through meadows, broadleaf woodland and alongside follies and former industrial sites such as the reclaimed Derwenthaugh Coke Works, soon to be a landscaped park. It links with several other trails at its southern end.

 The route: Swalwell Visitor Centre (Blaydon) – Winlaton Mill – Rowlands Gill – Hamsterley – Ebchester – Consett

Distance: 11 miles one way, 22 miles both.

Category: Railway path.

Start and Parking: Swalwell Visitor Centre, beside Blaydon Rugby Club, sign-

The Family Cycling Trail Guide

posted off the A694 and the B6317 between Blaydon and Dunston (west of Newcastle-upon-Tyne). Also at Rowlands Gill, Pontburn Wood, Ebchester, Shotley Bridge and Lydgetts Junction.

 Surface + Hills: Fine gravel path. Gradual climb Southwest from Swalwell.

Roads + Road crossings: 4 busy roads are crossed and a short section (0.25 mile) on road at Rowlands Gill (turn left at first road junction past the garage and right at junction going into housing estate. Bump up the kerb, past the old station building block and follow the narrow track through the trees until you dip down onto the trail).

Links to other trails: From the Lydgetts Junction (Consett) end of the trail there are links to the **Lanchester Valley Walk**, **Waskerley Way** and the **Consett–Sunderland Path**. The last two of these form part of Sustrans C2C Route. From the Swalwell end the trail links to the **Keelman's Way**.

Cycle Hire:
Weardale Mountain Bikes, tel: 01388 528129.

 Map + Leaflet: OS Landranger Map 88. A fine set of laminated route cards covering 7 railway paths in County Durham can be purchased from The Countryside Group, Environment & Technical Services Dept., Durham County Council, County Hall, Durham. DH1 5UQ. Tel: 0191 383 4144. The *City Slicker* range of family cycling guidebooks to the region can be bought at local bookshops, including the Newcastle Map Centre, Grey Street, Newcastle, tel: 0191 261 5622.

 Refreshments: Pubs in Rowlands Gill, Ebchester and Shotley Bridge. Cafe at campsite in Rowlands Gill.

Nearest Railway: Gateshead Metro Centre.

77. DOVE VALLEY TRAIL, southwest of Barnsley, South Yorkshire

Once the line of the former Worsbrough Bank Railway, the trail follows the Dove Valley, an attractive tree-lined route on the outskirts of Barnsley, passing alongside Worsbrough Country Park.

 The route: Silkstone – Dodsworth – Worsbrough Mill and Country Park – Wombwell.

Distance: 7.5 miles one way, 15 miles both.

Category: Railway path.

Start + Parking: Worsbrough Country Park, just off the A61 to the south of Barnsley.

 Surface + Hills: Stone and gravel path. Steady climb from Wombwell westwards to Silkstone.

Links or other nearby trails: The Dove Valley Trail is part of the Trans Pennine Trail which will run from Southport to Hull.

 Map + Leaflet: OS Landranger Map 110. Leaflet available from Planning Services, Central Offices, Kendray Street, Barnsley. S70 2TN. Tel: 01226 772566.

 Refreshments: In Silkstone, Worsbrough and Wombwell.

Nearest Railway: Silkstone or Wombwell.

78. DOWNS LINK,
south of Guildford, Surrey

As its name suggests, this railway path route links the **North Downs Way** *(which is part footpath and part bridleway /byway) with the* **South Downs Way** *which is a long distance bridleway and a good challenge for mountain bikers. It is worth cycling the Downs Link in May when the woods south of the Thurlow Arms pub are carpeted with a display of bluebells.*

 The route: Bramley (on the A281 south of Guildford) – Cranleigh – Rudgwick – Slinfold – Southwater – Partridge Green – Henfield – Bramber (on the A283 north of Shoreham-by-Sea).

Distance: Anything up to 26 miles one way, 52 miles round trip.

Category: Railway path with some bridle-way sections.

Start + Parking: Bramley and Wonersh Old Station car park, south of Guildford. At the junction of the A281 and B2128, exit the roundabout towards 'Wonersh, Shamley Green'. After 200 yds turn left signposted 'Bramley Business Centre, Bramley and Wonersh Railway Station'. Also at Cranleigh (the far corner of the main car park, off the High Street, near the NatWest Bank). At the southern end, use Southwater Country Park

 .Surface + Hills: Mainly stone and gravel path. Some bridleway sections. Mud in winter and after prolonged rain. One climb south of The Thurlow Arms pub at Baynards (south of Cranleigh).

Roads + Road crossings: Several minor roads and one busy road to cross – the A281 south of Rudgwick. Road section near Christ's Hospital School, between Slinfold and Southwater.

Links or other nearby trails: The **South Downs Way** is a 100 mile bridleway between Winchester and Eastbourne. There is a waymarked trail in **Alice Holt Forest**, southwest of Farnham. The **Worth Way** and **Forest Way** start in East Grinstead.

 Map + Leaflet: OS Landranger Maps 186, 187 + 198.

Refreshments: Pubs and occasional tea shops in each of the towns /villages along the way.

Nearest Railway: Shalford, Horsham, Shoreham.

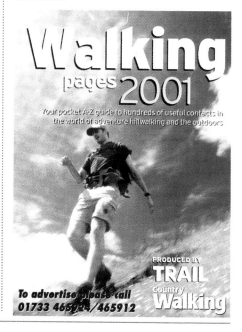

GALLOWAY
FOREST PARK

79 – 99 DUMFRIES & GALLOWAY FORESTRY
(21 routes in the Ae, Carrick, Clatteringshaws, Dalbeattie, Glentrool, Kirroughtree, and Mabie Forests)
There are over 200 miles of waymarked routes through the vast forestry holdings in Southwest Scotland so there is always something to suit every ability.

DISTANCE	MARKERS	GRADE	START & CAR PARK
A. FOREST OF AE. Tel: 01387 860247			
79. Windy Hill			
10 miles	Green	Easy	Glen Ae car park,
80. Upper Ae			A701, north of Dumfries
15 miles	Red	Moderate	
B. CARRICK FOREST. Tel: 01655 770618			
81. Barr to Loch Doon (linear route)			
19 miles	Red	Hard	Barr (B734, east of Girvan). Or Loch Doon (S. of Dalmellington)
C. CLATTERINGSHAWS LOCH. Tel: 01671 402420			
82. Clatteringshaws Loch			
14 miles	Green	Easy	Clatteringshaws Forest Wildlife Centre, on the A712 west of New
83. Craignell Hill			Galloway
15 miles	Purple	Moderate	
84. Deer Range			
9 miles	Blue	Hard	
85. Benniguinea Viewpoint			
4 miles	Red	Hard	
D. DALBEATTIE FOREST. Tel: 01671 402420			
86. Moyle Hill			
7 miles	Green	Easy	Richorn car park, A711 south of
87. Ironhash Hill			Dalbeattie
11 miles	Purple	Moderate	
E. GLENTROOL FOREST. Tel: 01556 503626			
88. Minniwick			
5 miles	Red	Easy	Glentrool Visitor Centre. A714
89. Balunton Hill			north of Newton Stewart
7 miles	Blue	Moderate	
90. Palgowan			
8 miles	Green	Moderate	
91. Borgan			
10 miles	Purple	Moderate	
F. KIRROUGHTREE FOREST. Tel: 01556 503626			

92. Palnure Burn

4 miles	Blue	Easy	Kirroughtree Visitor Centre, A75

93. Larg Hill

7 miles	Green	Moderate	east of Newton Stewart

94. Dallash

10 miles	Purple	Moderate

95. Old Edinburgh

18 miles	Red	Moderate

G. MABIE FOREST. Tel: 01387 860247

96. Woodhead

4 miles	Green	Easy	The Old Quarry, A710 south of

97. Craigend Hill

8 miles	Purple	Moderate	Dumfries

98. Lochbank

10 miles	Blue	Moderate

99. Marthrown Hill

3.5 miles	Red	Very hard!

 Surface + Hills: Forestry tracks. Tough climbs on harder routes.

Roads + Road crossings: Some of the routes use sections of quiet public roads.

Links or other nearby trails: The Sustrans Carlisle to Inverness Route passes through the forest. Other forestry routes in **Craik Forest** and the **Tweed Valley**.

Cycle Hire: At Mabie and Kirroughtree (see telephone numbers on previous page).

 Map + Leaflet: OS Landranger Maps 76, 77, 78, 83 + 84. Leaflets available from the forest offices listed above.

Nearest Railway: Dumfries or Girvan.

100. DYKE RAILWAY TRAIL,
Hove, Sussex

A useful escape from the built up coastal belt from Hove, near to Brighton, up onto the glorious South Downs, with a bridge crossing over the A27.

 The route: Hangleton (north Hove) north to Devils Dyke (on the South Downs Way).

Distance: 2 miles one way, 4 miles both.

Category: Railway path.

 Start + Parking: Car park at Devil's Dyke, off the A27 / A23 to the north of Hove.

Surface + Hills: Stone and gravel path. 230 ft climb from Hangleton to the Dyke.

Roads + Road crossings: None.

Links or other nearby trails: South Downs Way.

 Map + Leaflet: OS Landranger Map 198. Leaflet from Dept Planning, Borough of Hove, Town Hall Hove, BN3 4AH. Tel: 01273 775400.

 Refreshments: Pub at Devils Dyke.

Nearest Railway: Hove.

100a. EBURY WAY, Rickmansworth

A former railway line which links West Watford and Rickmansworth, crossing the Colne, Chess and Gade rivers as well as the Grand Union Canal.

 The route: Rickmansworth – West Watford

Distance: 3 miles one way, 6 miles round trip.

Category: Railway path.

Start + Parking: Five car parks in Rickmansworth; none close to the end of the trail at West Watford.

 Surface + Hills: Flat.

Roads + Road crossings: None.

 Map + Leaflet: Leaflet from Three Rivers District Council, tel: 01923 776611

 Refreshments: Plenty in both Rickmansworth and West Watford.

Nearest Railway: Rickmansworth

101. EGGESFORD FOREST, northwest of Exeter

With a forestry policy of planting a wide variety of trees and prudent thinning rather than wholesale cutting, the various woodlands of Eggesford Forest have achieved a harmonious mixture of deep forest and open glade.

 The route: Waymarked forest trail starting from the Garden Centre.

Distance: 6 miles.

Category: Forestry trail.

Start + Parking: Eggesford Garden Centre, on the A377, 20 miles northwest of Exeter.

 Surface + Hills: Stone / gravel path, occasional rough sections. Several short, steep hills.

Roads + Road crossings: Road section between the Garden Centre and the start of the woodland trail. Short section on quiet lane at the end of the Heywood Wood loop.

Links or other nearby trails: The Tarka Trail starts in Petrockstowe, 12 miles to the west.

Cycle Hire: Eggesford Country Cycle Hire. Tel: 01769 580250.

 Map + Leaflet: OS Landranger Maps 180 + 191. Leaflet available from Forest Enterprise, Bullers Hill, Kennford, Devon. EX6 7XR. Tel: 01392 832262.

 Refreshments: At the garden centre.

Nearest Railway: Eggesford.

101a. ELAN VALLEY TRAIL, Rhayader, mid-Wales

This is a new converted railway line cyclepath that navigates its way past four Victorian dams and reservoirs. The former railway line was created by the Birmingham Corporation Railway company, which tells you where the water from the reservoirs was bound.

 The route: Waymarked route starting from Caban Coch dam.

Distance: 6 miles one way, minor roads can be used on the way back.

Category: Railway path.

Start + Parking: Elan Valley Visitor Centre, 4 miles from Rhayader on the B4518.

 Surface + Hills: Flat stone/gravel path.

Roads + Road crossings: None

Links or other nearby trails: Lôn Las Cymru links in with the Elan Valley Trail.

Cycle Hire: Elan Cyclery, tel: 01597 811343

 Map + Leaflet: OS Landranger map 147. Leaflet available from the Elan Valley Visitors Centre, Rhayader, LD6 5HP, tel: 01597 810880.

Nearest railway: Llandrindod Wells (15 miles)

ELGIN – see 184–188. North East Scotland Forestry

102. EPPING FOREST, N of London

 One of London's green lungs, Epping Forest has dozens of miles of tracks through the woodland. No specific route is described. It is best to turn up with a map and explore!

Category: Forest trails.

Start + Parking: Epping Forest Conservation Centre, near High Beach, off the A104 between Chingford and Epping.

 Surface + Hills: Good stone-based paths. May be muddy after prolonged rain. Several small hills.

Roads + Road crossings: Several major road crossings.

Links or other nearby trails: The Lee Navigation runs to the west.

 Map + Leaflet: OS Landranger Maps 167 + 177. Maps are also available at the Visitor Centre at High Beach. Tel: 0191 508 0028.

 Refreshments: Several pubs dotted around Epping Forest.

Nearest Railway: Chingford, Loughton, Epping.

103. ESSEX FOREST PARKS
There are cycling possibilities in several of the country parks in Essex along the trails marked for horses. The quality varies and they are best avoided after prolonged rain.

Belhus Woods 73 hectares	**M25 Jct 30** 01708 865628	
Cudmore Grove 43 hectares	**S of Colchester** 01206 383868	
Hadleigh Castle 185 hectares	**E of Basildon** 01702 551072	
Hainault Forest 119 hectares	**NW of Romford** 0181 500 7353	
Langdon Hills 136 hectares	**S of Basildon** 01269 542066	
Thorndon 151 hectares	**S of Brentwood** 01277 211250	
Weald 195 hectares	**W of Brentwood** 01277 261343	

104. FIVE PITS TRAIL, southeast of Chesterfield
The trail follows the course of the railway that used to serve the collieries, passing through rolling countryside with fine views. There are a couple of hills which may come as a surprise to anyone expecting railway paths to be flat!

The route: Grassmoor – Holmewood – Tibshelf – Tibshelf Ponds – Highfields (crossing of the A6175) – Grassmoor.

Distance: 6 mile circuit plus 7 mile round trip to Tibshelf Ponds ie 13 miles total.

Category: Railway path.

Start + Parking: The Birkin Lane car park between Temple Normanton and Grassmoor, southeast of Chesterfield. Take the A617 Mansfield Road out of Chesterfield for 4 miles. Turn off south onto the B6245, then take the B6039, following signs for Temple Normanton and Holmewood. Turn second right. The car park is 0.75 of a mile along this road on your right.

Surface + Hills: Good gravel tracks. Fairly steep climb near the start of the trail. Second climb near to Tibshelf.

Roads + Road crossings: The busy A6175 is crossed twice and the B6039 once.

Links or other nearby trails: The Pleasley Trails lie just to the east. The Staveley to Killamarsh Trail lies 6 miles to the north.

Map + Leaflet: OS Landranger Map 120.

Refreshments: The Wheatsheaf, Tibshelf.

Nearest Railway:
Alfreton, south of the route.

105. FLITCH WAY, Braintree, Essex
The best of Essex's dismantled railways with the option of a good pub at Little Dunmow, at the western end of the ride. (The trail continues west beyond Little Dunmow for 1.5 miles to

the A130 south of Great Dunmow).

PS 'Flitch' is an old term for a large piece of bacon and refers to a wedding present given as a medieval incentive in Essex for a couple to get married rather than live in sin. The Flitch ceremony was held at the parish church in Little Dunmow.

The route: Braintree – Rayne – Little Dunmow.

Distance: 7 miles one way, 14 miles return.

Category: Railway path.

Start + Parking: Braintree Railway Station car park (the end furthest from the station).

Surface + Hills: Fine gravel path and no hills of note.

Roads + Road crossings: The crossing of the horrendously fast A120 just west of Rayne is avoided by taking the signposted alternative south of the old Rayne station, using quiet lanes. A quiet minor lane leads to the pub in Little Dunmow.

Links or other nearby trails: South of Bishop's Stortford, the **Stort Navigation** runs towards London. **Epping Forest** has many miles of fine tracks.

Map + Leaflet: OS Landranger Map 167 .

Refreshments: Lots of choice in Braintree, Flitch of Bacon pub in Little Dunmow.

Nearest Railway: Braintree.

106. FOREST OF DEAN FAMILY TRAIL, Gloucestershire
A very popular waymarked woodland trail in one of the largest forests in the West Country.

The route: Waymarked circular route through the forest.

Distance: 12 miles.

Category: Railway path and forestry tracks.

Start + Parking: Pedalabikeaway Cycle Centre, Cannop, just east of Coleford, tel: 01594 860065. The centre is 1 mile north of the crossroads formed by the B4226 and the B4234.

 Surface + Hills: Stone and gravel path. Several climbs.

Roads + Road crossings: The B4234 is crossed at the start and finish. The B4226 is crossed once. Care should be taken at each crossing.

Links or other nearby trails: There are plenty more tracks to explore in the forest. On the other side of the Severn there is the **Stonehouse – Nailsworth Railway Path** and the **Sharpness & Gloucester Canal** as well as the **Bristol & Bath Railway Path**.

Cycle Hire: At the Pedalabikeaway Centre. Tel: 01594 860065.

 Map + Leaflet: OS Landranger Map 162. Leaflet can be purchased from Forest Enterprise, Bank House, Bank Street, Coleford, Glos. GL16 8BA. Tel: 01594 833057.

 Refreshments: At the start or at Speech House Hotel.

Nearest Railway: Lydney.

107. FOREST WAY,
east of East Grinstead, Sussex
The countryside around Hartfield is the setting

of A.A. Milne's Winnie the Pooh stories so watch out for Tiggers and Heffalumps! This is an open ride through arable land lying between the High Weald to the south and the North Downs to the north.

 The route: East Grinstead (College Lane / A22 roundabout) – Forest Row – Hartfield – B2110 (1 mile west of Groombridge).

Distance: 9 miles one way, 18 miles both.

Category: Railway path.

Start + Parking: The car park on College Lane / De La Warr Road on the east of East Grinstead (on the town centre side of the roundabout on the A22 Eastbourne Road). From the car park return to De La Warr Road and turn right. At the T–junction with College Lane turn right for 100 yards then first left downhill by a stone wall. At the end of Old Road, cross to the opposite pavement, turn left then right through fence onto path. At the next road go straight ahead onto Forest Way.

 Surface + Hills: Stone and gravel path. No hills.

Roads + Road crossings: Short road section at the start in East Grinstead. One busy road to cross – the A22 just north of Forest Row.

Links or other nearby trails: The **Worth Way** starts from East Grinstead Railway Station car park.

 Map + Leaflet: OS Landranger Maps 187 + 188.

 Refreshments: Lots of choice in East Grinstead. Good pubs just off the route in Hartfield, Withyham and Groombridge.

Nearest Railway: East Grinstead.

108. FORTH & CLYDE CANAL, between Glasgow and Edinburgh
With the opening of Sustrans Clyde to the Forth Route there will be two ways of cycling between Scotland's major cities on largely traffic-free routes. The Forth & Clyde Canal towpath starts to the west of Glasgow and ends just short of Grangemouth.

NB Please read *The Waterways Code – Cycling on the towpath* at the back of this book

 The route: Bowling – Clydebank – northern edge of Glasgow – Kirkintilloch – Kilsyth – Bonnybridge – Falkirk – Grangemouth.

Distance: Up to 42 miles one way, 84 miles round trip.

Category: Canal towpath.

Start + Parking: The canal joins the Clyde just off the A82 between Clydebank and Dumbarton, 1.5 miles west of the Erskine Bridge (A898). It follows the route listed above and ends between Falkirk and Grangemouth, just to the west of the M9 Junction 6.

 Surface + Hills: Good gravel path, occasional muddy sections after rain. No hills.

Links or other nearby trails: The towpath links with the **Glasgow – Loch Lomond Trail** at its western end, crosses the **Strathblane to Kirkintilloch Path (Strathkelvin Railway Walkway)** in Kirkintilloch, and runs very close to the **Union Canal** in Falkirk.

 Map + Leaflet: OS Landranger Map 64 + 65.

 Refreshments: All along the way.

Nearest Railway: There are railway stations on or close to the route along its entire length.

FORT WILLIAM – see 281. West of Scotland Forestry

109. FRISTON FOREST, west of Eastbourne, East Sussex.
Two rides starting from Exceat, where the River Cuckmere has cut a course through the chalk ridge of the South Downs. A short ride goes to the coast and back. The longer ride is a way-marked forest route.

 The route: Waymarked route heading east, north then southwest through Friston Forest. There is also a track running parallel with the Cuckmere River out to the coast.

Distance: Forest circuit – 4.5 miles. To the coast and back – 2 miles.

Category: Forest trail and stone track through Seven Sisters Country Park.

Start + Parking: Car park in Exceat, on the minor lane towards Litlington, just off the A259 to the east of Seaford. The trail starts from the corner of the car park (signposted 'Country park /Living World') by some wooden 'claws' sculptures.

 Surface + Hills: Stone–based forest road, short sections of grassy track. One climb in the forest, none to the sea.

Roads + Road crossings: The busy A259 must be crossed if you wish to follow the track through Seven Sisters Country Park to the sea. Cross by the bus stop, signposted 'To the beach, Foxholes'. TAKE CARE.

Links or other nearby trails: The Cuckoo Trail starts at Polegate, 4 miles north of Eastbourne. The South Downs Way is a long distance bridleway that runs from Winchester to Eastbourne.

Cycle Hire: Cuckmere Cycle Co., Friston Forest, Tel: 01323 870310.

 Map + Leaflet: OS Landranger Map 199.

 Refreshments: Pubs in Friston, Jevington and Litlington.

Nearest Railway: Berwick or Polegate

110. FULBOURN ROMAN ROAD, southeast of Cambridge

This ride uses a short section of the old Roman Road that used to be known as Woles or Wolves Street and linked Colchester with Godmanchester. It should only be ridden in the summer months as it will be muddy in winter or after prolonged rain.

 The route: Car park on the minor road southwest of Fulbourn – Worsted Lodge (crossing of the A11) – B1052 (between Linton and Balsham).

Distance: 6.5 miles one way, 13 miles both.

Category: Track along the course of an old Roman Road.

Start + Parking: Small car park 2 miles southwest of Fulbourn along the minor lane known as Shelford Road. If starting from Cambridge, take the A1307 road towards Haverhill then turn left on the outskirts of town, just after the roundabout by Addenbrooke's Hospital onto the Fulbourn Road. The car park is 1.5 miles along on your right.

 Surface + Hills: Chalk track, at times rough. Muddy in winter. Several gentle hills.

Roads + Road crossings: The A1 is crossed via a bridge. If you want refreshment in either Linton or Balsham you will need to spend time on public roads. (Look at the map for the best minor roads to use).

Links or other nearby trails: Grafham Water is 20 miles to the west. Thetford Forest lies 25 miles northeast.

 Map + Leaflet: OS Landranger Map 154.

 Refreshments: In Fulbourn, Balsham or Linton (all 2 miles off the route).

Nearest Railway: Cambridge or Great Shelford.

GALLOWAY FOREST PARK – see 79 – 99. Dumfries & Galloway Forestry

111. GARWNANT FOREST, north of Merthyr Tydfil, South Wales

Lying just north of the old industrial town of Merthyr Tydfil, in Garwnant you are in a completely different world of woodland, lakes and reservoirs in this forestry holding on the southern edge of the Brecon Beacons National Park.

 The route: Two waymarked loops in the forest, starting from the Visitor Centre.

Distance: 5 miles or 10 miles.

Category: Forest trail.

Start + Parking: Garwnant Visitor Centre, just off the A470, 6 miles north of Merthyr Tydfil.

Surface + Hills: Forest tracks. Several hills, some steep.

Roads + Road crossings: A short section of a minor road is used in both routes.

Links or other nearby trails: The Taff Trail runs from Cardiff to Brecon and passes through Merthyr Tydfil.

Cycle Hire: At the Visitor Centre. Tel: 01685 723060.

 Map + Leaflet: OS Landranger Map 160. A leaflet can be purchased from the Visitor Centre. Tel: 01685 723060.

 Refreshments: At the Visitor Centre.

Nearest Railway: Merthyr Tydfil.

112. GISBURN FOREST, north of Clitheroe, Lancashire

 There are three waymarked trails in this small forestry holding north of Clitheroe.

Category: Waymarked forest trails.

Start + Parking: Cocklet Hill, on the minor road which crosses the B6478 Slaidburn – Long Preston road 4 miles northeast of Slaidburn.

 Surface + Hills: Forest tracks. Some hills.

Roads + Road crossings: None

Links or other nearby trails: The River Lune Cycleways start in Lancaster

 Map + Leaflet: OS Landranger Map 103.

 Refreshments: None en route.

Nearest Railway: Long Preston.

113. GLASGOW TO THE BANKS OF LOCH LOMOND

One of several routes out of Glasgow, this one links the Lowlands with the start of the Highlands on the bonny, bonny banks of Loch Lomond.

 The route: Bell's Bridge, central Glasgow – Clydebank – Bowling – Dumbarton – River Leven – Balloch – Loch Lomond.

Distance: 19 miles one way, 38 miles both.

Category: Railway path, canal towpath, riverside path.

Start + Parking: The path starts at Bell's Bridge (near to the Scottish Exhibition & Conference Centre, just west of the M8 Jct 20). Do you *really* need to take a car? There are many railway stations on this route, with frequent services. Many of the stations are very close to the cycle route.

 Surface + Hills: Fine gravel path. No hills.

Roads + Road crossings: Short sections of road are used through Dumbarton.

Links or other nearby trails: This is part of Sustrans Carlisle to Inverness National Cycle Network Route. At Bell's Bridge in Glasgow, you can link to the **Johnstone to Greenock** and **Johnstone to Kilbirnie Routes**.

 Map + Leaflet: OS Landranger Maps 63 + 64.

Refreshments: Lots of choice along the way.

Nearest Railway: Railway stations all along the way.

GLENTROOL – see 88 – 91. Dumfries & Galloway Forestry

114. GLOUCESTER & SHARPNESS CANAL, Gloucestershire

The canal links the River Severn with itself! The river is subject to such high tides that a canal was built to connect Gloucester, the limit of the tidal section, with the wider Severn Estuary at Sharpness.

 The route: Sharpness Docks – Purton – Frampton on Severn – Quedgeley – Hempsted Bridge (southwest edge of Gloucester).

Distance: 15 miles one way, 30 miles both.

Category: Canal towpath.

Start + Parking: Frampton on Severn, on the B4071 to the west of Stroud (M5 Jct 13) is a good place to start.

 Surface + Hills: Some rough and rutted sections. No hills.

Roads + Road crossings: No dangerous crossings.

Links or other nearby trails: The Stonehouse to Nailsworth Cycle Trail. Bristol & Bath Railway Path.

 Map + Leaflet: OS Landranger 162.

 Refreshments: Several pubs along the way.

Nearest Railway: Cam & Dursley Station.

115. GRAFHAM WATER, SW of Huntingdon

One of the few round reservoir routes in the country, this is well-signposted and very popular, particularly during summer weekends.

 The route: West Perry (just off the A1 between St Neots and Huntingdon) – circuit of Grafham Water.

Distance: 10 miles.

Category: Round reservoir route.

Start + Parking: There are three main pay and display car parks – Mander Park, Plummer Park and Marlow Park. Best to do the route anti–clockwise.

 Surface + Hills: Stone and gravel path. Some gentle hills where the trail leaves the waterside.

Roads + Road crossings: One short road section through West Perry on the south side of the lake.

Links or other nearby trails: The country's most famous reservoir route, **Rutland Water**, lies 30 miles to the north. The **Brampton Valley Way** (Northampton – Market Harborough) lies 25 miles W.

Cycle Hire: Grafham Water Cycling in Marlow Car Park. Tel: 01480 812500.

 Map + Leaflet: OS Landranger Map 153. The cycle hire centre also has maps.

Refreshments: Cafes in Mander and Marlow Parks. Pubs in Grafham and West Perry.

Nearest Railway: Huntingdon.

116. GRAND UNION CANAL from London to Daventry

One of the best escapes from London (see also **Lee & Stort Navigation, Thames Towpath***), the Grand Union Canal towpath can be followed for over 100 miles towards Birmingham. It is not a route for speed – there are lots of walkers, anglers and barriers!*

 The route: London (Ladbroke Grove) – Uxbridge – Rickmansworth – Watford – Hemel Hempstead – Tring – Leighton Buzzard – Milton Keynes – (SW of Northampton) – Norton Junction (NE of Daventry).

Distance: 110 miles.

Category: Canal towpath.

Start: Ladbroke Grove (near the Sainsbury's supermarket), Kensal Town, London. Beyond Uxbridge the surroundings become much greener.

 Surface + Hills: Stone-based path, of varying quality and width. No hills.

Roads + Road crossings: None.

Links or other nearby trails: **Thames Towpath, Milton Keynes Redway, Brampton Valley Way** (Northampton – Market Harborough).

 Map + Leaflet: OS Landranger Maps 152, 165, 166 + 176. You may prefer to use the Nicholson *Ordnance Survey Guide to the Waterways. 1: South.*

 Refreshments: All along the way.

Nearest Railway: All along the way.

117. GRAND WESTERN CANAL, Tiverton, Devon

One of two sections of canal towpath that are used in the Sustrans West Country Way, the long distance trail that runs from Padstow to Bristol. This route follows the WCW along a mixture of railway path, minor road & towpath.

 The route: Blundells Road / Western Way (B3391) Tiverton – Halberton – Sampford Peverell – Westleigh – Whipcott.

Distance: 10 miles one way, 20 miles both.

Category: Railway path and canal towpath.

Start + Parking: Blundells Road, on the eastern edge of Tiverton, near the roundabout with Western Way / Heathcote Way (B3391). Alternative starts in Halberton, Sampford Peverell or Westleigh.

 Surface + Hills: Tarmac, stone and gravel path, some muddy sections after rain. No hills.

Roads + Road crossings: Sections of minor road are used through Halberton and Sampford Peverell.

Links or other nearby trails: The **Bridgwater & Taunton Canal** is also on the West Country Way. The **Quantocks Ridge** is a good challenge for mountain bikes.

 Map + Leaflet: OS Landranger Map 181. Sustrans West Country Way map can be purchased from Sustrans, 35 King Street, Bristol. BS1 4DZ. Tel: 0117 929 0888.

Refreshments: Lots of choice in Tiverton. Pubs in Halberton and Sampford Peverell.

Nearest Railway: Tiverton.

118. GREAT GLEN CYCLE ROUTE from Fort William to Inverness

One of the most spectacular long distance routes in the country using a mixture of minor roads and forestry tracks, passing alongside several lochs. Remember to wave at Nessie on your way past Loch Ness!

The route: Fort William – Gairlochy – Loch Lochy – Invergarry – Loch Oich – Fort Augustus – Loch Ness – Drumnadrochit – Inverness.

Distance: 80 miles.

Category: Long distance route on mixture of surfaces.

Surface + Hills: Tarmac, forestry roads.

Roads + Road crossings: The route uses several sections of minor roads and a longer section of the A82 near to Inverness.

Links or other nearby trails: See North of Scotland Forestry Routes and Northeast Scotland Forestry Routes.

Map + Leaflet: OS Landranger Maps 26, 34 + 41. *Great Glen – Cycling in the Forest* leaflet available from: Forest Enterprise, Strathoich, Fort Augustus, Inverness–shire. PH32 4BT. Tel: 01320 366322.

Refreshments: In each of the main villages along the way.

Nearest Railway: Inverness or Fort William.

119. GRIZEDALE FOREST, southwest of Ambleside, Lake District

The main forestry area in the Lake District with several waymarked trails.

Start + Parking: At the Visitor Centre, on a minor road 4 miles southwest of Hawkshead.

Surface + Hills: Forestry tracks. Several hills.

Roads + Road crossings: The minor road between Hawkshead and Satterthwaite is crossed on some of the routes.

Links or other nearby trails: Whinlatter Forest, west of Keswick, also has waymarked forest trails.

Cycle Hire: At the Visitor Centre. Tel: 01229 860 369.

Map + Leaflet: OS Landranger Map 97. Leaflet (£1 + p&p) from Forest Enterprise, Lakes Forest District, Grizedale, Hawkshead, Ambleside. LA22 0QJ. Tel: 01229 860369. Fax: 01229 860273. Visitor Centre, tel: 01229 860010.

Refreshments: At the Visitor Centre. Pub in Satterthwaite.

Nearest Railway: Windermere.

120. GUISBOROUGH FOREST, south of Middlesbrough

Forestry Commission holding which stretches up the steep escarpment of the North York Moors to the south of the town of Guisborough. This route combines an easy railway path trail with a tougher challenge in the hills.

Distance: Railway path 3 miles (6 miles round trip) plus a 5 mile waymarked (blue markers) forest circuit.

Category: Railway path and forest trails.

Start + Parking: Pinchinthorpe car park, to the west of Guisborough, just south of the junction of the A173 with the A171.

 Surface + Hills: The railway path is flat with a good surface. The forest trails are steeper and rougher (mountain bikes recommended).

Roads + Road crossings: Short section (0.75 mile) on quiet road through Hutton.

Links or other nearby trails: Castle Eden Walkway, N of Stockton–on–Tees. **Dalby Forest** lies 20 miles southeast.

 Map + Leaflet: OS Landranger Maps 93+ 94. Leaflet available from Forest Enterprise. Tel: 01751 72771.

 Refreshments: Guisborough.

Nearest Railway: Nunthorpe, 1 mile west.

121. GWYDYR FORESTRY COMMISSION, Betws y Coed, North Wales
Two waymarked forest trails in this highly popular tourist area. There are also plans to develop Trailquest in one part of the woods. This is a form of orienteering where you are challenged to use your navigational skills to find various waymarks through the forest.

 The route: Two waymarked forestry trails starting from Betws y Coed.

Distance: 8 and 11 miles.

Category: Forest trails.

Start + Parking: Betws y Coed, near the junction of the A470 and A5 on the western edge of Snowdonia. There are long stay car parks in the village. Best to arrive early during busy periods. The northern trail starts by the car park /toilets on the minor road leading west off the B5106. For the southern trail you must follow the A5 towards Bangor for 0.5 mile. The route starts soon after the Miners Arms pub. For the clearest waymarking, ride anti-clockwise.

 Surface + Hills: Forest tracks.

Roads + Road crossings: Both routes use sections of minor roads. The southern route starts by using a 0.5 mile stretch of the A5.

Links or other nearby trails: Two railway paths start in **Caernarfon**. There are more waymarked forestry routes in **Coed y Brenin Forest**, 25 miles to the south.

Cycle hire: Beics Betws. Tel: 01690 710766.

 Map + Leaflet: OS Landranger Map 115. Much better is the Forestry Commission map of Gwydyr Forest which can be bought at the Information Centre or from: Forest Enterprise, Gwydyr Uchaf, Llanrwst, Gwynedd. LL26 0PN. Tel: 01492 640578.

 Refreshments: Lots of choice in Betws y Coed.

Nearest Railway: Betws y Coed.

122. HADDINGTON TO LONGNIDDRY, east of Edinburgh
One of several railway paths lying close to Edinburgh. East Lothian is a very progressive authority and there will eventually be a safe link for cyclists from Longniddry, along the coast to Musselburgh and thence into the centre of Edinburgh.

 The route: West side of Haddington (Alderston Road) – Longniddry railway station.

Distance: 4.5 miles one way, 9 miles both.

Category: Railway path.

Start + Parking: The route starts on Alderston Road, on the west side of Haddington (near to the hospital). From the centre of Haddington follow signs for Edinburgh. Alderston Road is a street on your right towards the end of the village. Or start from Longniddry railway station.

 Surface + Hills: Stone and gravel path. No hills.

Roads + Road crossings: You will need to use roads to get to the start of the trail in Haddington.

Links or other nearby trails: The Pencaitland Railway Walk lies 7 miles to the southwest. The **Dalkieth to Penicuik Cycleway** is a little further west.

 Map + Leaflet: OS Landranger Map 66.

 Refreshments: Haddington and Longniddry.

Nearest Railway: Longniddry.

HADRIAN'S WAY
– see **North Tyne Cycleway**

123. HAMSTERLEY FOREST,
southwest of Durham
Several waymarked trails in this popular destination for recreational cyclists. Hamsterley Forest covers an area of 2000 hectares with a mixture of broadleaf and coniferous woodlands.

Distance: Three waymarked trails of 4, 7 and 11 miles.

Category: Forestry trails.

Start + Parking: Hamsterley Forest Visitor

Centre, 1 mile from Hamsterley village, 15 miles southwest of Durham. A toll is payable on the road from Bedburn to the Visitor Centre.

 Surface + Hills: Tarmac, hills, forestry tracks, mountain bikes recommended.

Roads + Road crossings: The routes follow the Forest Drive for a part of their length so expect light traffic.

Links or other nearby trails: The **Auckland Walk** and the **Brandon and Bishop Auckland Trail** start from Bishop Auckland.

Cycle Hire: Weardale Mountain Bikes, tel: 01388 528 129. Hamsterley Forest Bike Hire. Tel: 01388 528129.

 Map + Leaflet: OS Landranger Map 92. Forest Enterprise leaflet available at the Visitor Centre. Tel: 01388 528129.

 Refreshments: Refreshment kiosk at the Visitor Centre. Pub in Hamsterley village.

Nearest Railway: Bishop Auckland, 9 miles to the east.

124. HARLAND WAY,
southeast of Harrogate
Follow this railway path from the market town of Wetherby through lush countryside to the village of Spofforth with its medieval castle.

 The route: The old station in Wetherby to Spofforth.

Distance: 3.5 miles one way (plus 1 mile to reach Spofforth Castle) ie 9 miles round trip from Wetherby to Spofforth Castle.

Category: Railway path.

Start + Parking: Old station car park, Linton Road, Wetherby. Follow the A661 from the centre towards Harrogate. Bear left at first junction to Linton.

 Surface + Hills: Stone and gravel path. No hills.

Roads + Road crossings: One busy road to cross (A661) to visit Spofforth Village and its castle.

Links or other nearby trails: There are two trails starting in **York**.

Cycle Hire: Spa Cycles, 1 Wedderburn Road, Harrogate. Tel 01423 887003.

 Map + Leaflet: OS Landranger Map 104.

 Refreshments: Lots of choice in Wetherby. Railway Inn in Spofforth.

Nearest Railway: Harrogate.

125. HART TO HASWELL WALKWAY, north of Hartlepool
Fine railway path with good views of the coast and the Cleveland Hills.

 The route: Hart Station (on A1086 north of Hartlepool) – Hesleden – Shotton Colliery – Haswell.

Distance: 9 miles one way, 18 miles both.

Category: Railway path.

Start + Parking: Hart Station, just off the A1086 between Hartlepool and Blackhall Colliery. Or Hesleden, Castle Eden Inn, Shotton Colliery (old station) Haswell.

 Surface + Hills: Fine gravel path from Hart to Castle Eden. West from here the trail is grassier and rougher: MTBs recommended. No hills.

Roads + Road crossings: Three road crossings, including the busy A181 north of Wingate.

Links or other nearby trails: The **Brandon & Bishop Auckland Walk**, the **Auckland Way, Deerness Valley Walk,** and **Lanchester Valley Walk** all lie less than 10 miles to the west. The **Consett & Sunderland Cycleway** lies 10 miles to the north.

 Map + Leaflet: OS Landranger Maps 88 + 93.

 Refreshments: Pubs along the way in each village.

Nearest Railway: Hartlepool, 4 miles southeast of Hart Station.

126 –127 HIGH PEAK AND TISSINGTON TRAILS, Peak District
Two of the best known and most popular routes in the country offering a superb challenge in the heart of the Peak District. The trails form the shape of an inverted wishbone, linking in the north at Parsley Hay. If you start here, remember it is all downhill on the way out so you will be faced with a climb on your return.

 The Route:
1. Tissington Trail: Ashbourne – Tissington – Parsley Hay.
2. High Peak Trail: High Peak Junction (south of Matlock) – Middleton Top – Parsley Hay – Sparklow.

Distance:
1. Tissington Trail 13 miles one way, 26 miles round trip.
2. High Peak Trail 17.5 miles one way, 35

miles round trip. The flattest section runs for 12 miles between Middleton Top and Parsley Hay.

Category: Railway paths.

Starting points and parking: Parsley Hay is where the two trails meet and there is a large pay and display car park and cycle hire centre. Otherwise:

1. Tissington Trail – car parks on the B5054 east of Hartington; on the A515 near Alsop; on the minor road east of Thorpe; or Mapleton Lane in Ashbourne.

2. High Peak Trail – car parks at Friden (near the junction of the A515 and A5012); Middleton Top Visitor Centre (southwest of Matlock on the B5035 towards Ashbourne); Black Rock (north of Wirksworth on the B5036); and High Peak Junction (on the A6 south of Matlock).

 Surface: Excellent stone paths.

Hills:
1. Tissington Trail: There is a steady drop of almost 700 ft (215 mts) from Parsley Hay to Ashbourne. For this reason it is worth con-sidering starting at Ashbourne when you are fresh, riding uphill to Parsley Hay, leaving you with a downhill on the way back.

2. High Peak Trail: The top section from Sparklow through Parsley Hay to Middleton top is fairly flat. After that it drops over 800 ft (245 mts) in little over 2 miles with some very steep sections. Ensure your brakes are in good condition.

Roads + Road crossings: The A5012 must be crossed close to Friden on the High Peak Trail.

Other nearby trails: Carsington Water, the **Monsal, Manifold** and **Churnett Valley Trails** are all nearby.

 Cycle Hire:
Parsley Hay. Tel: 01298 84493
Middleton Top. Tel: 01629 823204.
Ashbourne. Tel: 01335 343156.

 Map + Leaflet: OS Landranger Map 119. Peak Cycle Hire. Leaflet available from: Information Group, Peak National Park Office, Aldern House, Baslow Road, Bakewell, Derbyshire. DE4 1AE. Tel: 01629 816220.

Refreshments:
1. Tissington – plenty of choice in Ashbourne. Soft drinks and sweets at the cycle hire / Visitor Centres. Pubs just off the route in Thorpe (Dog & Partridge) and Biggin (Waterloo Inn). Coffees and teas at Basset Wood Farm, Tissington.

2. High Peak – Soft drinks and sweets at the cycle hire / Visitor Centres. Royal Oak pub at Hurdlow (north of Parsley Hay). Pub just off the route in Middleton (Rising Sun).

Nearest Railway: Matlock, Buxton or Uttoxeter.

128. HOPTON MOUNTAIN BIKE TRAIL, west of Ludlow, Shropshire
The whole of the wood has been waymarked enabling you to devise your own route with the help of the Forest Enterprise leaflet (see details below). Please note that it is very hilly and steep and only suitable for fit cyclists!

 The route: With the aid of the leaflet, plan your own route.

Distance: For a small forestry holdng there are several miles of forest roads and single track.

Category: Forest trails.

Start + Parking: Hopton Castle, west of

Ludlow. Follow the A4113 west of Ludlow then the B4385 and a minor road north and west through Hopton Castle to the car park in Hopton Titterhill Wood.

 Surface + Hills: Forest roads, single track. Lots of steep climbs and descents.

Roads + Road crossings: None.

 Map + Leaflet: OS Landranger Map 137. The leaflet is essential for this forest. It can be purchased from: Forest Enterprise, Marches Forest District, Whitcliffe, Ludlow, Shropshire. SY8 2HD. Tel: 01889 586593.

 Refreshments: In Bucknell, south of the forest.

Nearest Railway: Hoptonheath.

129. HOUGHTON FOREST, north of Arundel, West Sussex.
Forestry route with superb views from the downland edge section.

 The route: Waymarked forest route from Whiteways Lodge roundabout, north of Arundel.

Distance: 3 miles. Follow the green cycle pictograms.

Category: Forest trail.

Start + Parking: Whiteways roundabout, at the junction of the A29, A284 and the B2139, 4 miles to the north of Arundel.

 Surface + Hills: Forest tracks. Hills

Roads + Road crossings: None.

Links or other nearby trails: There are more waymarked trails in **Queen Elizabeth Country Park** near to Petersfield. The **South Downs Way** runs for 100 miles from Winchester to Eastbourne. Some of the ridge sections are suitable for family cycling.

 Map + Leaflet: OS Landranger Map 197. A leaflet is produced covering this route and two others. The pack is called 'Three Offroad Routes on the Chichester Downland' and can be purchased from: County Planning Officer, West Sussex County Council, County Hall, Tower Street, Chichester PO19 1RL Tel: 01243 777610.

 Refreshments: Kiosk at the roundabout.

Nearest Railway: Amberley.

130. HUDSON WAY from Beverley to Market Weighton, northwest of Hull
Explore the gently rolling hills of the southern Yorkshire Wolds, linking the historic towns of Beverley and Market Weighton.

 The route: Beverley – Market Weighton (northwest of Hull).

Distance: 11 miles one way, 22 miles return.

Category: Railway path.

Start + Parking:
1. Beverley. Car park just off the A1035 Beverley bypass to the north of the town.
2. Market Weighton. Old station site, north of Station Road, off St Helen's Square behind the parish church.

 Surface + Hills: Stone/gravel path, grass. No hills.

Roads + Road crossings: Several minor roads, one busy road to cross – the B1248 north of Cherry Burton. Take great care at this point.

Links or other nearby trails: At its western end it links to the **Market Weighton to Bubwith Trail**. Two nearby trails start from Hull – **Hull to Hornsea** and **Hull to South Holderness**.

 Map + Leaflet: OS Landranger Maps 106 + 107.

 Refreshments: Lots of choice in Beverley and Market Weighton. Cafe in Kiplingcotes Station. Pubs just off the route in Goodmanham and Etton.

Nearest Railway: Beverley Station.

131. HULL TO SOUTH HOLDERNESS

Starting close to the centre of Hull, the railway path runs to the north of the Humber Estuary almost to the village of Patrington with its magnificent church known as 'The Queen of Holderness'.

 The route: Southcoates Lane (north of Alexandra Dock / Hedon Road / Prison) Hull – Hedon – Keyingham – A1033 just west of Patrington.

Distance: 13 miles one way, 26 miles both.

Category: Railway path.

Start + Parking: Southcoates Lane, Hull (north of Alexandra Dock, HM Prison), Hedon or Patrington.

 Surface + Hills: Gravel and grass. Rough sections at the eastern end. No hills.

Roads + Road crossings: Minor roads from the centre of Hull. Two short sections of quiet lanes. Patrington is 1 mile beyond

the end of the railway path along the A1033 (take care).

Links or other nearby trails: The **Hull to Hornsea Trail** also starts in the centre of Hull.

 Map + Leaflet: OS Landranger Map 107. Hull Cycle Map available from: Department of Environmental Services, Essex House, Manor Street, Hull. HU1 1YD. Tel: 01482 593346.

 Refreshments: Hull, Hedon, Patrington.

Nearest Railway: Hull.

132. HULL – HORNSEA TRAIL

Follows the line of the old railway across Holderness from the centre of Hull to Hornsea.

 The route: Hull – New Ellerby – Hornsea.

Distance: 13 miles one way, 26 miles both.

Category: Railway path.

Start + Parking: Dansom Lane, off Holderness Road, just east of Hull City Centre, and just west of the junction of Holderness Road with Mount Pleasant.

 Surface + Hills: Tarmac or good gravel path. No hills.

Roads + Road crossings: You have to cross several minor roads and the A165 south of Skirlaugh. Roads in Hull and Hornsea.

Links or other nearby trails: The **Hull to Holderness Trail** also starts from Hull.

 Map + Leaflet: OS Landranger Map 107. Hull Cycle Map available from: Dept. of Environmental Services, Essex House, Manor

Street, Hull. HU1 1YD. Tel: 01482 593346

 Refreshments: Hull and Hornsea. The Railway Inn near the old station in Ellerby.

Nearest Railway: Hull.

133. INNOCENT RAILWAY, Edinburgh
Good exit from the heart of Edinburgh out to the east. The trail starts from the edge of the magnificent Holyrood Park.

 The route: St Leonard's Bank, Edinburgh (at the southwest corner of Holyrood Park) – Duddingston Loch – Bingham – Brunstane.

Distance: 4 miles one way, 8 miles both.

Category: Railway path.

Start + Parking: St Leonard's Bank, Newington (near the Royal Commonwealth Pool, at the SW edge of Holyrood Park).

 Surface + Hills: Fine gravel path.

Roads + Road crossings: Several minor roads to cross.

Links or other nearby trails: Water of Leith, Union Canal, Newbridge & Forth Road Bridge, Dalkieth to Penicuik, Pencaitland Railway Walk.

 Map + Leaflet: OS Landranger Map 66. Much better is a street map of Edinburgh or better still the SPOKES cyclists map of Edinburgh which can be purchased from Lothian Cycle Campaign, St. Martins Church, 232 Dalry Road, Edinburgh EH11 2JG, tel: 0131 313 2114.

 Refreshments: Edinburgh

Nearest Railway: Waverley Station, Edinburgh or Musselburgh.

133a JERSEY: CORBIERE WALK
This is possibly the prettiest former railway path in the country with a stunning destination: the lighthouse at Corbiere. The Walk – now used more by cyclists than walkers – is lined in parts with palm tress and other exotic flora.

 The route: from St Aubin to the Corbiere lighthouse

Distance: 3.5 miles one way, 7 miles both.

Category: Railway path.

Start + Parking: The start is next to St Aubin harbour, near Market Street, straight on from the small Nat West bank. Parking is available in St Aubin and at various car parks close to the promenade starting at St Helier. This promenade is open to cyclists (but watch out for the trackless tourist train!)

 Surface + Hills: Gravel path. There's a 2 mile climb from St Aubin to St Brelade ('traffic-calmed' to prevent you hitting terminal velocity on the way back).

Roads + Road crossings: 5 minor road crossings.

Links to other trails: There are no other truly traffic-free waymarked routes on Jersey but the Corbiere Walk crosses many points of access on to the Green Lane network where cars are discouraged with 15 mph speed restrictions.

Cycle Hire: Jersey Cycletours tel: 01534 482898; Zebra Cycle Hire, tel: 01534 36556

 Map + Leaflet: from Jersey Tourism, Liberation Square, St. Helier, tel: 01534 500700.

 Refreshments: Plenty of pubs and cafes in St. Aubin. Along the way is the Poplars tea room, La Moye, St Brelade (tel 01534 42184). This is in a farmhouse owned by the Bissan family since 1690. Coming back from the light-house it's a right turn at the first road crossing.

Nearest Railway: none

Special Focus on...

The largest and most southerly of the Channel Islands is a paradise for cyclists because of 'Green Lanes' where cars are discouraged, and bikes welcomed!

JERSEY

...JERSEY

Cycle heaven

With only one waymarked off-road trail – the 3.5 mile Corbiere Walk – Jersey shouldn't really be included in a book of traffic-free trails. Except, that is, Jersey has a unique and innovative green credential. It has a 15mph speed limit on 40 miles of small country roads.

Jersey has a superb network of tarmaced 'Green Lanes', leafy roads meandering between fields of Jersey cows to and from granite farmhouses and cottages. Since first mooted in 1986 and the erection of the first signposts in 1994, these Green Lanes – which the States of Jersey, the local government, classify as 'particular attractive or of great character and antiquity' – have been protected from speeding motorists by the imposition of the cycle-friendly speed limit.

When motorists do venture along Green Lanes – and only a determined few can be bothered – they find their way impeded at every turn by locals and tourists walking and cycling in the middle of the road.

Despite having one of the highest per capita car ownership levels in Europe, the backroads of Jersey are surprisingly free of fast-moving traffic.

The main round-island ring road is extremely busy, but even in peak periods the Green Lanes are havens of peace and tranquillity.

Many of the finest Green Lanes have become part of the new Jersey cycle network, parts of which are open and way-marked right now with the remainder scheduled for completion later in 2000.

This network was surveyed by John Grimshaw, director of Sustrans, the rails-to-trails construction charity. He was extremely impressed with the cycle tourism potential of the island: "There is nowhere in the United Kingdom to compare with Jersey when it comes to cycling. Its network of quiet, rural lanes, its varied and beautiful countryside, its small scale and clement weather all make an encouraging framework to take up cycling as your way to explore and discover the Island."

On your beach
And after meandering along a Green Lane – having demolished a Jersey cream tea along the way – what better than to end up on one of Jersey's sandy bays. Unlike British and Mediterranean resorts, no untreated sewage is allowed into the sea. The effluent treatment plant at Bellozanne uses ultra violet light to disinfect final sewage ensuring clean beaches and bathing water.

In the 1997 Marine Conservation Society's *Good Beach Guide*, twelve of Jersey's bays achieved the highest Four Dolphin rating. The society is fulsome in its praise: "With 55kms of coastline, ranging from high cliffs to sweeping bays, and bathing waters which rate the highest EU standards, Jersey must count as a prime location for the discerning beach lover."

On your bike
With Jersey's commitment to providing for cyclists and all the many attractions for the whole family, such as the world-famous conservation zoo founded by Gerald Durrell, and the German Underground Hospital, the island has a lot going for it.

For more details call Jersey Tourism on 0345 055 055 and ask for the new cycle map of Jersey, £1.00.

JERSEY FACTS: did you know...?

● Jersey is 100 miles south of mainland Britain, three and a half hours away from Poole by ferry. France is 14 miles away and can be seen from Jersey on all but the dullest of days. Of which there aren't many on Jersey: the island has one of the best sunshine records in the British Isles with average summer temperatures of 20C.

● **The island – 9 by 5 miles – packs a lot into its 45 square miles, including the large sandy bays of the south and west coasts; the rocky beaches of the east; the quiet meadows and valleys of the interior; and the rugged grandeur of the north coast.**

● Jersey is neither part of the UK nor a colony, but is still part of British Isles. Jersey is not represented in Parliament at Westminster. There are no political parties on Jersey. Government is carried out by the Jersey Parliament – the States Assembly – and involves committees made up from 53 elected independent members.

● **In addition to its official police force (remember Bergerac?) Jersey also has a unique unpaid, non-uniformed police force which has operated since Norman times. Local 'constables' have official – and draconian – powers. There are no speed cops on the 15mph Green Lanes but transgressors may be arrested by Constables.**

● Cyclists holidaying on the island in July or September should pack plenty of spare inner tubes. The custom of branch and hedge trimming – or branchage – leads to copious roadside thorns. Some cycle hire fleets on Jersey come equipped with puncture proof 'solid' tyres to combat this problem. The *visites du branchage* is an official inspection of the distance from the road or footpath of overhanging foliage. Landowners with errant trees are fined, hence the zealous trimming and copious thorns.

134. JOHNSTONE TO GREENOCK, west of Glasgow

Although there is a waymarked route right into the heart of Glasgow it is very bitty between Johnstone and Glasgow and uses several sections of roads. By contrast the Johnstone to Greenock route is almost entirely on the course of an old railway line.

 The route: Johnstone – Bridge of Weir – Kilmacolm – Port Glasgow – Greenock (Lady Octavia Recreation Centre).

Distance: 14 miles one way, 28 miles both.

Category: Railway path.

Start + Parking: The ride starts in Johnstone where Old Road passes beneath the railway, just off the B789 (Main Road), 1 mile to the west of the roundabout at the junction of the B789 with the A761. Alternative starting points in Bridge of Weir, Kilmacolm, Port Glasgow and Greenock.

 Surface + Hills: Fine gravel path. One hill in Port Glasgow.

Roads + Road crossings: Short sections of roads in Kilmacolm and Port Glasgow.

Links or other nearby trails: Links with the **Johnstone to Kilbirnie Route.**

 Map + Leaflet: OS Landranger Maps 63 + 64. Leaflet available from Strathclyde Roads, Strathclyde Regional Council, Richmond Exchange, 20 Cadogan Street, Glasgow. G2 7AD. Tel: 0141 227 2581.

 Refreshments: Johnstone, Bridge of Weir, Kilmacolm, Port Glasgow, Greenock.

Nearest Railway: Johnstone or Whinhill Station, Greenock.

135. JOHNSTONE TO KILBIRNIE

The second of two dismantled railways that run west from Johnstone. This one takes a more southerly direction, passing Castle Semple Loch, Barr Loch and Kilbirnie Loch along its course.

 The route: Johnstone – Lochwinnoch – Kilbirnie.

Distance: 11 miles one way, 22 miles both.

Category: Railway path.

Start + Parking: The ride starts in Johnstone where Old Road passes beneath the railway, just off the B789 (Main Road), 1 mile to the west of the roundabout at the junction of the B789 with the A761. Alternative starting points in Lochwinnoch (Castle Semple Visitor Centre) or Kilbirnie.

 Surface + Hills: Fine gravel path. No hills.

Roads + Road crossings: Several minor roads to cross.

Links or other nearby trails: The trail links with the **Johnstone to Greenock Route.**

 Map + Leaflet: OS Landranger Maps 64 + 65. Leaflet available from: Strathclyde Roads, Strathclyde Regional Council, Richmond Exchange, 20 Cadogan Street, Glasgow. G2 7AD. Tel: 0141 227 2581.

 Refreshments: Johnstone, Kilmacolm, Kilbirnie.

Nearest Railway: Johnstone, Kilbirnie.

136. KEELMAN'S WAY, Gateshead (South Tyne Cycleway)

*Running along the south side of the Tyne from Hebburn and Gateshead across the county border and into Northumberland. It can easily be linked to the **North Tyne Cycleway.***

The Route: Wylam – Blaydon – Dunston – Gateshead – Bill Quay – Hebburn Riverside Park.

Distance: 14 miles one way, 28 miles both.

Category: Railway path.

Start + Parking: Car parks in Wylam and Hebburn.

 Surface + Hills: Tarmac or gravel path. No hills.

Roads + Road crossings: Several short road sections – east of Newburn Bridge, east of Blaydon Haughs Industrial Estate, at Derwenthaugh Marina, Dunston and Friars Goose Marina. The route is well–signposted throughout. If you want a shorter, completely traffic–free route, cross Newburn Bridge and return to Wylam via the North Tyne Cycle Way.

Other nearby trails: links to North Tyne Cycle Way and Derwent Valley Walk. The latter in turn links to the Consett and Sunderland Railway Path, the Waskerley Way and the Lanchester Way. A section of the Keelman's Way is used on Sustrans C2C Route which crosses the country from the Cumbrian Coast at Whitehaven (or Workington) to the East Coast at Tynemouth or Sunderland.

Cycle Hire: Newcastle Cycle Centre, 165 Westgate Road, Newcastle upon Tyne. Tel: 0191 222 1695.

 Map + Leaflet: OS Landranger Map 88. Keelman's Way leaflet available from Planning Dept, Gateshead MBC, Civic Centre, Regent Street, Gateshead. NE8 1HH. Tel: 0191 477 1011.

 **Refreshments:** All along the way.

Nearest Railway: Wylam, Blaydon, Hebburn.

137. KENNET & AVON CANAL TOWPATH from Bath to Hungerford

One of the longest sections of canal towpath open to cyclists in the whole country. See the spectacular viaducts at Avoncliff and Dundas and the amazing flight of locks at Caen, near Devizes.

PERMIT: In the summer of 1997 the canal authority introduced a £12.50 yearly permit (free for under 16's). This is available from British Waterways, Bath Road, Devizes SN10 1HB. Tel: 01380 722859. The policy is under review.

NB Please read *The Waterways Code – Cycling on the towpath* at the back of the book

 The route: Bath Spa Station – Bradford–on–Avon – Devizes – Hungerford.

Distance: 50 miles one way from Bath to Hungerford.

Category: Canal towpath.

Start + parking: Back of Bath Spa Railway Station, or any of the villages/towns along the way. But if arriving by car, avoid starting in Bath city centre, try Bathampton or Bradford-on-Avon instead.

 Surface + hills: Variable. From grassy to gravel path.

Roads + Road crossings: None, once you have found the start in Bath.

Other nearby trails: The Bristol & Bath

Railway Path starts on the western edge of Bath. The Ridgeway runs from near Avebury to Goring-on-Thames. The Marlborough–Chiseldon Railway Path. The canal towpath forms part of the National Cycle Network Route 4 from the Severn Bridge to Newbury.

Cycle Hire: Avon Valley Cyclery (back of Bath Spa railway station). Tel: 01225 461880 or 01225 442442.

 Map + Leaflet: OS Landranger Maps 172, 173, 174. Or for a comprehensive map of the whole canal send £4.25 to GEOprojects Ltd., 9–10 Southern Court, South Street, Reading RG1 4QS. Tel: 0118 939 3567.

 Refreshments: All along the way.

Nearest Railway: Bath Spa, Freshford, Bradford–on–Avon, Pewsey, Great Bedwyn, Hungerford.

138. KESWICK RAILWAY PATH, Lake District.

After negotiating the steps and gates beneath the A66 road bridge, this short, delightful trail crosses and recrosses the scenic River Greta towards Threlkeld. Here you have several options along quiet, attractive lanes to return to Keswick.

 The route: Old Railway Station, Keswick (near the Leisure Pool) – A66 on the outskirts of Threlkeld.

Distance: 4 miles one way, 8 miles return.

Category: Railway path.

Start + Parking: At the old station in Keswick (near the Leisure Pool).

 Surface + Hills: Gravel path. Steep steps and gates to negotiate where the trail passes beneath the A66 road bridge.

Roads + Road crossings: None unless you choose to go into Threlkeld for refreshments or to return via Castlerigg Stone Circle.

Links or other nearby trails: Keswick lies on the course of the C2C Route. There are waymarked trails in nearby Whinlatter Forest.

Cycle Hire: Keswick Mountain Bikes, Southey Hill, Keswick. 017687 75202.

 Map + Leaflet: OS Landranger Map 90.

 Refreshments: Lots of choice in Keswick. Pubs in Threlkeld.

Nearest Railway: Nowhere nearby. Penrith or Workington both 16 miles away.

139. KIELDER WATER, Northumberland

Kielder Water is the second largest manmade lake in Western Europe (the largest is at Rutland Water) and Kielder Forest is the largest man-made forest in Britain covering over 600 square kilometres. The circuit of the reservoir (half of which is on a public road) is just one of many waymarked routes in the area.

Distance: 17 miles, plus 6 miles for the excursion around Bullcrag Peninsula.

Category: Round reservoir route.

Start + Parking: Kielder Castle Visitor Centre, on the minor road west from Bellingham. (40 miles NW of Newcastle).

Surface + Hills: Minor road and stone forestry track. Several short climbs.

Roads + Road crossings: The southern half of the circuit is along the access road to Kielder Castle Visitor Centre.

Other nearby trails: There are 10 way-marked cycle routes in the forest, some of which are steep and challenging. See 'Map + Leaflet' below for details.

Cycle Hire:
Kielder Castle. Tel: 01434 253392.
Leaplish Waterside Park. Tel: 01434 250312.

 Map + Leaflet: OS Landranger Map 80. Leaflet (costs £2) showing routes in the Kielder Forest area is available from Forest Enterprise, Kielder Forest District, Ealsburn, Bellingham, Hexham, Northumberland. NE48 2AJ. Tel: 01434 220242.

 Refreshments: Cafe at Kielder Castle. Pub in Kielder village. Lakeside cafe at Leaplish Waterside Park, tel: 01434 250312

Nearest Railway: Hexham, 20 miles SE.

140. KINGSWINFORD RAILWAY TRAIL, southwest of Wolverhampton
A fine, well-maintained, wooded trail with a countryside feel that belies its proximity to the built-up areas of Wolverhampton.

 The route: Pensnett (west of Dudley on the A4101) – Himley – Wombourne – Castlecroft – Tettenhall – Aldersley Stadium.

Distance: 10 miles one way, 20 miles both.

Category: Railway path.

Start + Parking:
Wombourne. Turn off the A449 Wolverhampton to Kidderminster road at the roundabout near Wombourne where the A463 joins the A449 signposted 'Kingswinford Railway Walk. Trysull, Seisdon'. Follow signs for Trysull onto Billy Buns Lane then just before a brown and cream railway bridge turn right onto a track signposted 'Kingswinford Railway Walk'.

 Surface + Hills: Good quality stone and gravel track. No hills.

Roads + Road crossings: None.

Links or other nearby trails: The **Birmingham & Black Country Canal Towpath** runs from the centre of Birmingham to the centre of Wolverhampton.

 Map + Leaflet: OS Landranger Map 139.

 Refreshments: Excellent tea shop at Wombourne Station. Pubs just off the route.

Nearest Railway: Wolverhampton.

KIRROUGHTREE FOREST – see 92 – 95. Dumfries and Galloway Forestry

141. LANCHESTER VALLEY WALK, northwest of Durham
The trail runs between Durham and Consett, following the River Browney to Lanchester then Backgill Burn to Howns Gill Viaduct across predominantly arable land.

 The route: Broompark car park (B6302, west of Durham) – Langley Park – Lanchester – A692, south of Consett.

Distance: 12 miles one way, 24 miles both.

Category: Railway path.

Start + Parking: Broompark picnic site, south of Durham. From the A617 take the A690 towards Crook then first right on the B6302. The car park is signposted to the left. Also at Langley Park, Malton, Lanchester and Hownes Gill Viaduct.

 Surface + Hills: Fine gravel path. Gradual climb into Consett.

Roads + Road crossings: Several minor road crossings.

Links or other nearby trails: Lots! From Broompark car park to the **Deerness Valley Walk** and **Brandon to Bishop Auckland Walk**. From Consett to the **Waskerley Way, Consett to Sunderland Railway Path** and the **Derwent Walk**.

Cycle Hire: Weardale Mountain Bikes, tel: 01388 528129.

 Map + Leaflet: OS Landranger Map 88. A fine set of laminated route cards covering 7 railway paths in County Durham can be purchased from The Countryside Group, Environment & Technical Services Dept., Durham County Council, County Hall, Durham. DH1 5UQ. Tel: 0191 383 4144.

 Refreshments: Lots of choice in Lanchester and Consett. Pub in Langley Park.

Nearest Railway: Durham Railway Station is 2 miles from Broompark car park.

LANGDALE FOREST, North York Moors – see **Dalby** or **Sneaton**
142. **LEE & STORT NAVIGATION,**

North London

A superb escape from North London into the countryside on a recently upgraded towpath which sets a fine example against which other towpaths should measure themselves.

 The route: Victoria Park (Hackney) – Hackney Marshes – Waltham Abbey – Broxbourne.

Distance: 17 miles one way, 34 miles both.

Category: Canal towpath.

Start + Parking: Victoria Park, Hackney. The southeast corner of the park at the junction of Cadogan Terrace and Jodrell Road. Follow the Hertford Union Canal to the junction with the Lee Navigation and turn left. Also at Lee Valley Country Park, Waltham Abbey.

 Surface + Hills: Fine gravel path, no hills.

Roads + Road crossings: None.

Links or other nearby trails: Epping Forest and the **Cole Greenway**.

Cycle Hire: Lee Valley Cycle Hire, Broxbourne Meadows, Mill Lane, Broxbourne. Tel 01992 630127.

 Map + Leaflet: OS Landranger Maps 166 and 176. You may prefer to use the Nicholson *Ordnance Survey Guide to the Waterways. 1: South.*

 Refreshments: Lots of choice along the way.

Nearest Railway: Several stations are close to the canal.

143. LEEDS & LIVERPOOL CANAL
along the Aire Valley, west of Leeds

Take a trip along the towpath of the oldest surviving Trans-Pennine waterway, exploring this green corridor along Airedale from the heart of Leeds out to Shipley.

 The route: Granary Wharf, in the centre of Leeds – Horsforth – Shipley.

Distance: 13 miles one way, 26 miles both.

Category: Canal towpath.

Start + Parking: Shipley railway station. Granary Wharf in Leeds.

 Surface + Hills: Good gravel path. No hills.

Roads + Road crossings: At the start and finish near to the railway stations.

Links or other nearby trails: The Aire & Calder Navigation runs southeast from Leeds city centre.

Cycle Hire: Watson Cairns & Co, Lower Briggate, Leeds. Tel: 0113 245 8081.

 Map + Leaflet: OS Landranger Map 104. Leaflet available from British Waterways, Pottery Road, Wigan WN3 5AA.

 Refreshments: Pubs at Apperley Bridge, Rodley and Newlay.

Nearest Railway: Leeds or Shipley.

144. LEICESTER GREAT CENTRAL WAY AND THE CANAL NETWORK

By combining a dismantled railway with a towpath and a riverside path it is possible to pass right the way through Leicester from the north (Watermead Country Park) to the south (Blaby)

on traffic-free routes or designated cycle lanes.

 The route: Watermead Country Park (Birstall) – Abbey Park – Great Central Way – Grand Union Canal – Crow Mill car park (on the southern edge of Leicester, on the road towards Countesthorpe).

Distance: 10 miles one way, 20 miles both.

Category: Railway path, riverside path, canal towpath.

Start + Parking: St Margaret's Pasture car park near the Sports Centre, just off St Margaret's Way (near Abbey Park in the centre of Leicester).

1. North to Watermead Park. Go round one and a half sides of the square formed by the sports ground, then turn right over the concrete river bridge and right again signposted 'Riverside Way / Birstall'. (Remember this point for your return). You will follow blue-and-white markers for the majority of the way. At T–junction with road cross via pelican crossing.

2. South to Blaby. From St Margaret's Pasture car park return to the main road and turn left down the steps on to the towpath.

 Surface + Hills: Fine gravel path on the central section. The track becomes a little rougher the further north or south you go. No hills.

Roads + Road crossings: The roads are crossed via pelican crossings.

Links or other nearby trails: Rutland Water, 20 miles to the east. The Brampton Valley Way 16 miles southeast.

Map + Leaflet: OS Landranger Map 140. A very useful booklet for the area is called *Cyclists' Leicester: Leicester Spokes Street by Street Guide to Environment City*. Costs £2.95 from Leicester Spokes, PO Box 30, Leicester LE1 7GD.

 Refreshments: Gazebo Cafe in the Abbey Grounds. White Horse pub, Birstall. The County Arms pub, Blaby.

Nearest Railway: Leicester.

145. LIVERPOOL LOOP LINE
(Halewood & Aintree)
The railway path runs along wooded embankments and between sandstone cuttings around the eastern edge of Liverpool. There are extensive views as far as the Pennine foothills.

 The route: Halewood (southwest of M62 Jct 6) – Knotty Ash – Walton.

Distance: 10 miles one way, 20 miles both.

Category: Railway path.

Start + Parking: Halewood Triangle Country Park, southwest of M62 Jct 6 or Walton Loop Line Nature Park (north Liverpool, west of M57 Jct 4).

 Surface + Hills: Mostly tarmac, some stone/gravel sections. No hills.

Roads + Road crossings: Several quiet roads to cross.

Links or other nearby trails: The **Cheshire Lines Path** starts 5 miles north of Walton (the northern end of the Liverpool Loop Line).

 Map + Leaflet: OS Landranger Map 108.

 Refreshments: At the Halewood Visitor Centre. Cafe and pubs in West Derby (Mill Lane). Pubs in Rice Lane.

Nearest Railway: Halewood/Broad Green /Rice Lane.

146. LIVINGSTON, west of Edinburgh
As with its southern counterpart, Milton Keynes, Livingston is a new town which has adopted a very progressive attitude towards cycling and there are close to 200 miles of dedicated cycle tracks in and around the town. Go with a map of the town (details below) and an open mind and you will be agreeably surprised!

 The route: Choose your own with the aid of the map. There are attractive sections alongside the Rivers Almond and Murieston.

Distance: There are nearly 200 miles of cycleways through Livingston.

Category: Network of urban cycleways.

Start + Parking: With the aid of the map you can start at the point which is most convenient for you.

 Surface + Hills: Tarmac paths. Several gentle hills.

Roads + Road crossings: Roads are crossed safely: this is the whole point of the network!

Links or other nearby trails: The **Water of Leith Walkway** runs from Balerno into Edinburgh. Balerno is 7 miles east of Livingston.

Map + Leaflet: OS Landranger Map 65. Of more use is the map which can be purchased from West Lothian Council. Tel: 01506 775296.

 Refreshments: Lots of choice.

Nearest Railway: Nether Williamston or Newyearfield.

147. LLANFOIST TO GOVILON
railway path, SW of Abergavenny
A short, scenic section of railway path near to Abergavenny. As an alternative to a there-and-back route you could use the network of quiet, steep and almost traffic-free lanes to return to the start.

 The route: Llanfoist – Govilon.

Distance: 3 miles one way, 6 mile return.

Category: Railway path.

Start + Parking: In a road called The Cutting, by the Post Office in Llanfoist, to the southwest of Abergavenny. At the cross-roads by the Llanfoist Inn turn right then shortly after the car saleroom and a street called The Cedars on the right take the next narrow tarmac track to the right (sign-posted as a no through road). Immediately turn left onto the old railway path.

 Surface + Hills: Fine gravel path. Gentle climb from Llanfoist to beyond Govilon.

Roads + Road crossings: Short section on road from the Post Office in Llanfoist to the start of the route. One minor road to cross.

Links or other nearby trails: Taff Trail runs through Talybont on Usk, 15 miles W

 Map + Leaflet: OS Landranger Map 161.

 Refreshments: In Llanfoist.

Nearest Railway: Abergavenny.

LOCHGILPHEAD – see **269 – 274**. **West of Scotland Forestry**

148. LOCH KATRINE, the Trossachs, north of Glasgow
This exploration of Loch Katrine is one of the loveliest rides in the whole book. There is a delightful tarmac track along along the north side of the loch which is open to walkers and cyclists but not vehicles. Unfortunately, there isn't a complete circuit of the lake.

 The route: The northern shore of Loch Katrine to its western end then the southern shore as far as Stronachlachar.

Distance: 10 miles one way, 20 miles both.

Category: Route along shoreline of loch.

Start + Parking: The pier car park at the eastern end of Loch Katrine at the terminus of the A821, to the west of Callander and the the north of Aberfoyle.

 Surface + Hills: Tarmac lane. Several hills.

Roads + Road crossings: The route uses a road but it is shut to traffic. If you wish to go on to Loch Lomond to the Inversnaid Hotel for refreshments you will need to use a road which carries some traffic (much more in the high season).

Links or other nearby trails: There are several waymarked forestry tracks in the **Queen Elizabeth Forest Park** in the vicinity of Aberfoyle and Callander. There is a traffic-free route from **Aberfoyle to Callander.**

 Map + Leaflet: OS Landranger Maps 56 + 57.

 Refreshments: At the Captain's Rest Cafe at the start. The Inversnaid Hotel, on the east shore of Loch Lomond, lies 5 miles to the west of Stronachlachar (ie this would add another 10 miles to the trip).

Nearest Railway: Glasgow and Dunblane, both more than 20 miles away.

149. LONGDENDALE TRAIL, east of Manchester

The route runs along the side of Longdendale past a string of reservoirs lying at the bottom of the valley. The scenery is spectacular, if a little spoiled by the line of pylons that runs parallel with the trail.

 The route: Hadfield – parallel with B6105 – Woodhead Tunnels (A628) – Dunford Bridge

Distance: 10 miles one way, 20 miles both.

Category: Railway path.

Start + Parking: Trail car park in Hadfield. Turn off the A57 Manchester to Glossop road just south of Hollingworth at the roundabout by the Spread Eagle pub and Woolley Bridge pub onto Woolley Bridge Road. At the next roundabout by The Lamp pub turn right onto Station Road towards the centre of Hadfield. Just before the railway bridge over the road there is a car park to the left at the start of the trail.

 Surface + Hills: Stone and gravel path. There is a 330ft climb from Hadfield to the Woodhead Tunnels.

Roads + Road crossings: The B6105 is crossed once; the busy A628 is crossed after the Woodhead Tunnels and again a mile after Audernshaw Clough.

Links or other nearby trails: The **Sett Valley Trail** runs between New Mills and Hayfield (south of Glossop on the A624). There is a trail around the edge of the **Upper Derwent Valley Reservoirs**. The Longdendale Trail is part of the **Transpennine Trail**, from Southport to Hornsea.

 Map + Leaflet: OS Landranger Map 110. Leaflet available from: North West Water, Bottoms Office, Woodhead Road, Tintwistle, Glossop SK13 1H. Tel 01457 864187.

 Refreshments: In Hadfield and there's a catering van at the Torside Visitor Centre halfway along the route.

Nearest Railway: Hadfield.

150. LUNE CYCLEWAYS, Lancaster

Follow the riverside cyclepath through Lancaster alongside the River Lune from the old port of Glasson Dock to the Crook o'Lune, the wide bend in the river just west of the village of Caton.

 The route: Glasson Dock (on the B5290 to the west of M6 Jct 33) – Lancaster town centre – Halton – Crook o' Lune.

Distance:
Lancaster – Glasson Dock 6 miles one way,
Lancaster – Crook o'Lune 5 miles one way,

Category: Riverside path.

Start and parking: Long Marsh Lane, Lancaster (down the hill from the railway side of Lancaster Castle). Lancaster city centre, near bus station. Glasson Dock car park at the end of the bike path. Crook o'Lune picnic site (signposted off the A683).

 Surface + Hills: The route west to Glasson Dock is rougher but both routes are being upgraded. No hills.

Roads + Road crossings: In Lancaster city centre.

Cycle Hire: Duke of Lancaster Cycle Hire. Tel: 01524 849484.

 Map + Leaflet: OS Landranger Map 97. County Publicity Department, Lancashire County Council, County Hall, Preston, Lancashire. PR1 8XJ. Tel: 01772 263399.

 Refreshments: Lots of choice in Lancaster. Pubs and cafe in Glasson Dock. Pub in Caton (just beyond Crook o'Lune).

Nearest Railway: Lancaster.

MABIE FOREST – see 96 – 99. Dumfries & Galloway Forestry

151. MANIFOLD TRAIL,
northwest of Ashbourne
One of the three most popular trails in the Peak District (along with the **High Peak** *and* **Tissington Trails**), *this scenic railway path follows the course of two rivers – the Manifold and the Hamps.*

 The route: Waterhouses (west of Ashbourne) – Wettonmill – Hulme End.

Distance: 8 miles one way, 16 miles both.

Category: Railway path.

Start + Parking:
1. Hulme End. 12 miles southwest of Bakewell. Turn off the B5054 just to the west of the Manifold Valley pub.

2. Waterhouses. 9 miles northwest of Ashbourne. Turn off the A523 Ashbourne to Leek road at Ye Olde Crown Hotel in Waterhouses, signposted 'Cauldon Lowe, Cheadle, Manifold Track'. Go under the bridge and immediately left into the car park. To get to the start of the trail go to the far end of the car park and follow the waymarks.

Surface + Hills: Tarmac or fine gravel path. The track dips in the middle, the junction of the Rivers Hamps and Manifold, so there is a gentle climb from this point (Weags Bridge) north to Hulme End or south to Waterhouses.

Roads + Road crossings: There is one busy road to cross at Waterhouses (the A523). The trail uses a short section of quiet lane for about 1.5 miles.

Links or other nearby trails: The **Tissington Trail** lies 4 miles to the east of Hulme End along the B5054. The **Churnet Valley Trail** (Oakamoor to Denstone) lies 6 miles south of Waterhouses.

Cycle Hire:
1. Peak National Park Cycle Hire, Waterhouses. Tel: 01538 308609.
2. Brown End Farm Cycle Hire, Waterhouses. Tel: 01538 308313.

Map + Leaflet: OS Landranger Map 119. Leaflet available from: Information Group, Peak National Park Office, Aldern House, Baslow Road, Bakewell, Derbyshire. DE4 1AE. Tel: 01629 814321.

Refreshments: The Manifold Valley pub at Hulme End. Various tea shops and refreshment vans along the way. Ye Olde Crown pub at Waterhouses.

Nearest Railway: Uttoxeter, 10 miles to the south.

152. MARKET WEIGHTON TO BUBWITH, southeast of York
One of two railway paths starting in or near Market Weighton, this one runs west to the village of Bubwith across the flat and fertile lands lying to the southwest of the Yorkshire Wolds.

 The route: Bubwith – Foggathorpe – (Holme on Spalding Moor) – A163 to the west of Market Weighton.

Distance: 12 miles one way, 24 miles both.

Category: Railway path.

Start + Parking: Bubwith village, on the A163 to the east of Selby. Take the minor road south from Bubwith towards Breighton. The railway path starts 0.5 mile along this road.

 Surface + Hills: Stone and gravel path. No hills.

Roads + Road crossings: Several minor road crossings, one busier road – the A163 between Holme and Foggathorpe.

Links or other nearby trails: The **Hudson Way** runs from Market Weighton to Beverley.

 Map + Leaflet: OS Landranger Map 106.

 Refreshments: In Market Weighton and Bubwith and just off the trail in Foggathorpe and Holme–on–Spalding–Moor.

Nearest Railway: Wressel,

153. MARLBOROUGH TO CHISELDON, south of Swindon
This railway path uses the course of the old Midland and Southwest Junction Railway that ran between Cheltenham and Southampton.

 The route: Marlborough (1 mile east of the town centre, on the A4 towards Hungerford) – Ogbourne St Andrew – Ogbourne St George – Chiseldon.

Distance: 7.5 miles one way, 15 miles both.

Category: Railway path.

Start + Parking: Figgins Lane Car Park by the River Kennet in Marlborough. Follow the pavement alongside the A4 towards Hungerford. Immediately after crossing the old railway bridge turn left into Barnfield. Or start at the car park just off the A346 to the south of Chiseldon.

 Surface + Hills: Stone and gravel path. Quality deteriorates north of Ogbourne St George. No hills.

Roads + Road crossings: A short section on lane through the small village of Ogbourne St George. Turn right 200 yds after the Old Crown Inn then right again onto Jubbs Lane to rejoin the railway path.

Links or other nearby trails: The trail crosses **The Ridgeway**. A traffic–free link is planned to the **River Ray Parkway** (Swindon) and to the **Kennet & Avon Canal.**

 Map + Leaflet: OS Landranger Maps 173 + 174.

Refreshments: Lots of choice in Marlborough. Old Crown Inn, Ogbourne St George.

Nearest Railway: Gt Bedwyn, 7 miles SE.

154. MARRIOTTS WAY, Norwich

Escape from the heart of Norwich into the countryside on one of the longest disused railways in the country. Easily links to the Weavers Way giving you the option of a challenging 60 mile round trip (Norwich – North Walsham – Norwich). The route is signposted as the Wensum Valley Walk from the centre of Norwich and becomes the Marriotts Way near to Drayton.

 The route: Norwich – Drayton – Themelthorpe – Reepham – Aylsham.

Distance: Up to 24 miles one way, 48 miles return.

Category: Railway path.

Starting points:
1. Aylsham (the Bure Valley Railway station).

2. Reepham – the Old Railway Station is 0.75 of a mile north of the centre of Reepham on the B1145 towards Aylsham (opposite the Crown pub).

3. Drayton (the trail crosses the A1067 between Drayton and Taverham).

4. Norwich (the roundabout by the River Wensum at the junction of Barn Road and St Crispins Road).

Parking: If arriving by car it is better to start in Reepham or Aylsham rather than drive into the centre of Norwich.

 Surface + Hills: Stone and gravel path, rough in places. No hills.

Roads + Road crossings: You will need to

use city streets from Norwich railway station/city centre to the start. Otherwise, several minor roads but only one busy road to cross (the A1067 near Drayton).

Links or other nearby trails: In Aylsham you can link to the **Weavers Way**, another dismantled railway that runs east to North Walsham. The **Peddars Way** lies 25 miles to the west and runs for 50 miles from near Thetford to the Norfolk Coast at Holme-next-the-Sea. The Marriotts Way forms part of Sustrans National Network Route 1 which runs 369 miles from Harwich to Hull.

Cycle Hire: At Reepham Station. Tel: 01603 871187.

 Map + Leaflet: OS Landranger Maps 133 + 134. Leaflet available from Department of Planning and Transportation, County Hall, Martineau Lane, Norwich. NR1 2SG. Tel: 01603 222230.

 Refreshments: Lots of choice in Aylsham, Reepham and Norwich and just off the route in Drayton and Lenwade.

Nearest Railway: Norwich Station (1.5 miles southeast of the start of the route) or North Walsham, which is on the **Weavers Way**, enabling you to cycle one way from Norwich to North Walsham (30 miles) and catch the train back.

MAWDDACH WALK – see 23.
Barmouth to Dolgellau

155. MEON VALLEY TRAIL, north of Fareham, Hampshire
A lovely long wooded trail through deepest Hampshire linking attractive villages with good watering holes.

The route: West Meon – Droxford – Soberton – Wickham.

Distance: 10 miles one way, 20 miles both.

Category: Railway path.

Start + Parking:
1. West Meon. Follow the A32 towards Wickham, passing the Red Lion pub. After 150 yds, on a sharp right hand bend, turn left onto Station Road then take the 1st track to the right. **Beware** of the height barrier if you have the bikes on the roof!

2. Droxford. Car park near the church / bus shelter. From the car park, cycle uphill away from the church and take Mill Lane on the right. Go downhill past the house alongside the stream then over the bridge. At the main road turn right then right again to go up onto the cycle track.

3. Wickham. From the main square in Wickham follow 'Free parking' signs out of town towards the A32. After 150 yards turn left onto Mill Lane then 1st right by the Fire Station onto Station Close and right again to park beneath the trees.

Surface + Hills: Stone and gravel path. Mountain bikes recommended. No hills.

Roads + Road crossings: No busy roads to cross. Short sections on roads to get to the pubs.

Links or other nearby trails: There is a waymarked forestry trail in **West Walk Forest**, northeast of Wickham and several forest trails in **Queen Elizabeth Country Park** near Petersfield.

Map + Leaflet: OS Landranger Maps 185 + 196.

Refreshments: Pubs in West Meon, Droxford, Soberton and Wickham.

Nearest Railway: Fareham, 4 miles south of Wickham.

156. MERSEY RIVER THROUGH SOUTH MANCHESTER

Follow the banks of the River Mersey through Sale Water Park amidst a landscape of flood plains and disused gravel pits, now a haven for wildlife.

The route: East Didsbury – riverbank of River Mersey – West Didsbury – Chorlton Water Park – Sale Water Park.

Distance: 6 miles one way, 12 miles both.

Category: Riverside path.

Start + Parking: The church in East Didsbury, just off the A5145 to the west of the A34 and to the north of M63 Jct 10.

Surface + Hills: Stone and gravel path. No hills.

Roads + Road crossings: None.

Links or other nearby trails: The **Middlewood Way** runs from Marple (east of Stockport) to Macclesfield.

Map + Leaflet: OS Landranger Map 109. A comprehensive cyclists' map of Manchester is produced by CycleCity Guides which shows all the city's recreational routes and best commuter routes. Available by sending £4.95 payable to CycleCity Guides, Wallbridge Mill, The Retreat, Frome BA11 5JU. Tel: 01373 453533.

Refreshments: At either end of the route.

Nearest Railway: Sale or East Didsbury.

157. MIDDLEWOOD WAY, East Cheshire

A fine long stretch of dismantled railway, much of it in woodland, running south from Marple (southeast Manchester) to Macclesfield, on the edge of the Peak District.

 The route: Marple (on the southeast outskirts of Manchester) – Higher Poynton – Bollington – Macclesfield.

Distance: 10.5 miles one way, 21 miles both.

Category: Railway path.

Start + Parking:
1. Next to the railway station in Macclesfield.

2. Adlington Road car park by the viaduct in Bollington, 3 miles northeast of Macclesfield, by the Dog & Partridge pub, signposted 'Middlewood Way' (or at the Cycle Hire Centre on Grimshaw Lane, Bollington).

3. Poynton Coppice and Higher Poynton, east of Poynton and the A523.

4. Two car parks in Higher Poynton: at Jackson's Brickworks and Nelson Pit.

5. Marple. Turn off the A626 Stockport to Glossop road in Marple, opposite the Rose Hill Post Office (close to the Railway pub) onto Railway Road, signposted 'Middlewood Way / Station car park' Look for a sign for the start of the Middlewood Way in the far left–hand corner of the car park.

 Surface + Hills: Mostly stone and gravel path, muddy in winter. No hills.

Roads + Road crossings: No dangerous crossings.

Links or other nearby trails: The **Sett Valley Trail** runs between New Mills and Hayfield, to the southeast of Marple. **Rudyard Lake** lies 10 miles south of Macclesfield. The **Biddulph Valley Line** starts form Congleton, 10 miles southwest of Macclesfield.

 Cycle Hire: Groundwork Trust, Grimshaw Lane, Bollington. Spring and summer weekends only. Tel: 01625 560050.

 Map + Leaflet: OS Landranger Map 109 + 118. *Pathways from the Past* leaflet available from Macclesfield Borough Council Ranger Service, Adlington Road, Bollington. Cheshire. 01625 573998 or Leisure Services 01625 504504. A comprehensive cyclists' map of Manchester is produced by CycleCity Guides which shows all the city's recreational routes and best commuter routes. Available by sending £4.95 payable to CycleCity Guides, Wallbridge Mill, The Retreat, Frome BA11 5JU. Tel: 01373 453533.

Refreshments: Lots of choice in Marple, Bollington and Macclesfield.

Nearest Railway: Marple, Middlewood and Macclesfield.

158. MILTON KEYNES REDWAY

There is an excellent network of recreational cycle routes around Milton Keynes, including circuits of lakes, tree-lined canal towpaths and well-made paths across parkland past Buddhist Pagodas.

 The route: Buy the Redway Map for the many options.

Distance: (Just one suggested route). 3 miles around Willen Lakes plus 7 miles along the Canal Broadwalk to Linford.

Category: Lakeside paths, canal towpaths, dedicated cycle network.

Start + Parking: Willen Lakes, just off the M1 Jct 14.

 Surface + Hills: Tarmac paths. The canal towpath is gravel-based. No hills.

Roads + Road crossings: None.

Links or other nearby trails: The **Grand Union Canal** runs from London to Birmingham.

 Map + Leaflet: OS Landranger Map 152. Much better is the Milton Keynes Redway Map (cost £1), available from Milton Keynes Tourist Information Centre, 890 Midsummer Boulevard, Central Milton Keynes, MK9 3QA. Tel: 01908 558300.

 Refreshments: Cafe at Willen Lakes Watersports Centre, pubs along the canal towpath.

Nearest Railway: Milton Keynes.

159. MONSAL TRAIL,
Bakewell, Peak District
Although the Monsal Trail runs for 9 miles from Bakewell towards Buxton, only a 4 mile section is open to cyclists. It is nevertheless well worth riding this fine trail through beautiful country-side in the southern Peak District.

 The route: Bakewell northwest to Little Longstone.

Distance: 5 miles one way, 10 miles both.

Category: Railway path.

Start + Parking: From the centre of Bakewell take the A619 towards Chesterfield. Immediately after crossing the bridge over the River Wye, turn first right onto Station Road, then right again onto Coombs Road – the pay and display long stay car park is second on right. To get to the railway path, turn right out of the car park for 3/4 mile then turn left steeply uphill just before the railway bridge. However there's now a kissing gate here which makes it difficult for tandems and trailers to get through. Easier access can be found at the car park just off the A6 between Bakewell and Matlock, about a mile out of Bakewell. Tel: 01629 816220.

 Surface + Hills: Broad, stone-based track.

Roads + Road crossings: The ride starts with a short section on a no through road with almost no traffic. You will need to use quiet lanes to get to the pubs at Little Longstone and Great Longstone.

Links or other nearby trails: The **High Peak** and **Tissington Trails** start 6 miles west of Bakewell at Parsley Hay.

 Map + Leaflet: OS Landranger Map 119. Leaflet available from: Information Group, Peak National Park Office, Aldern House, Baslow Road, Bakewell, Derbyshire. DE4 1AE. Tel: 01629 814321.

 Refreshments: Lots of choice in Bakewell. The Crispin pub, Great Longstone and the Pack Horse Inn, Little Longstone.

Nearest Railway: Buxton.

160. NEATH CANAL, between Neath and Glyn Neath, South Wales

There are plans for the whole length of the Neath Canal from Briton Ferry to Glyn Neath to be restored to its former glory. The section from Blaengwrach to Resolven, alongside the new stretch of the A465 shows what it could look like in the future. At present there are three rideable sections, the southern part is somewhat rougher.

The route (three sections):
1. Briton Ferry – Aberdulais
2. B4242, west of Glyn Neath to Resolven.
3. Clyne – Tonna – Neath.

Distance:
1. Briton Ferry to Aberdulais. 4 miles.
2. Northeast of Resolven. 3 miles one way, 6 miles round trip.
3. Southwest of Clyne. 4.5 miles one way, 9 miles round trip.

Category: Canal towpath.

Start + Parking:
1. The car park at the Resolven Basin just off the A465 to the north of Resolven.
2. In Clyne, Tonna or Neath.

Surface + Hills: Excellent stretch northeast of Resolven. The Clyne – Neath section has a mixture of surfaces, some fairly rough. No hills.

Roads + Road crossings: One in Tonna.

Links or other nearby trails: There are several waymarked trails from **Afan Argoed Country Park** on the A4107 to the north of Port Talbot.

Map + Leaflet: OS Landranger Maps 160 + 170.

Refreshments: Pubs in Resolven, Tonna. Pubs and cafes in Neath.

Nearest Railway: Neath.

161. NEWBRIDGE AND THE FORTH ROAD BRIDGE, west of Edinburgh

Linking the railway path between Newbridge and Queensferry with the cycletrack that runs along the side of the Forth Road Bridge. Not for those without a head for heights!

The route: Newbridge – Kirkliston – Dalmeny – Forth Road Bridge – North Queensferry.

Distance: 7 miles one way, 14 miles both.

Category: Railway path and bridge over Firth of Forth.

Start + Parking: East of Newbridge, just off the A8 to the east of the M8 Jct 2.

Surface + Hills: Tarmac cyclepath. Stone and gravel path. Climb up onto the bridge.

Links or other nearby trails: The **Water of Leith Walkway** from Balerno to Edinburgh.

Map + Leaflet: OS Landranger Map 65.

Refreshments: In Kirkliston, Queensferry and North Queensferry.

Nearest Railway: North Queensferry or Dalmeny.

162. NEW FOREST, Hampshire

In 1991 the Forestry Commission brought out a Cycling Code which encourages cycling as long as you stay on the 100 miles of waymarked gravel roads that criss-cross the area.

NOTE: the situation of cycling in the New

Forest is always precarious. The Verderers – New Forest guardians from the pre-medieval period – have it within their powers to greatly extend cycling possibilities in the New Forest but they are loath to do so for the fear of attracting rowdy mountain bikers.

Distance and category: There are 100 miles of forestry trails. You are encouraged to make up your own routes, as long as you stay on the gravel roads.

Start + Parking: There are over 140 car parks in the New Forest and tracks start from near all of them. If arriving by train, the best place to start is Brockenhurst. There is a cycle hire centre next to the station.

 Surface + Hills: Stone and gravel paths. Undulating.

Roads + Road crossings: Traffic is calmed throughout the New Forest so crossing the minor roads should not be a problem, although Brockenhurst can be busy.

Cycle Hire: New Forest Cycle Experience, The Island Shop, Brookley Road, Brockenhurst. Tel: 01590 624204.

 Map + Leaflet: OS Landranger Map 196. A leaflet called *Cycling in the Forest – the Network Map* showing all the forest tracks can be purchased from: Forest Enterprise, Queens House, Lyndhurst, Hants. SO43 7NH. Tel: 01703 28314. Or from the Tourist Information Centre in Lyndhurst. Tel: 01703 282269.

 Refreshments: Plenty of choice in Brockenhurst and Lyndhurst. Several pubs and hotels dotted around the New Forest.

Nearest Railway: Brockenhurst.

NEWPORT (ISLE OF WIGHT) – see 60. Cowes to Newport

163. NEWPORT TO CROSS KEYS CANAL, South Wales

One of two canals that run north from Newport. For such a built-up area the canal represents a fine green corridor with an excellent wide, gravel towpath and views of hills rising to over 1000 ft at its northern end.

 The route: Newport (Barrack Hill) – Risca – Cross Keys.

Distance: 9 miles one way, 18 miles both.

Category: Canal towpath

Start + Parking: Malpas Road (A4042), Newport. From M4 Jct 26 take the A4042 south towards Newport then park in one of the side streets to the right (Goodrich Crescent, Ross Lane, Walford Street). To get to the canal, follow Malpas Road for 200 yards south as far as the pedestrian bridge over the road. At this point turn right and keep bearing right to join the start of the canal towpath. Pass beneath a bridge then shortly you have a choice. At the next new stone bridge turn right beneath the M4 for Pontypool or continue straight ahead for Cross Keys. Or: the picnic site by the Fourteen Locks just off the B4591 to the north of M4 Jct 27.

 Surface + Hills: Gravel path. Gradual climb from Newport to Cross Keys with one steep section at locks.

Roads + Road crossings: Several minor roads to cross. Short section on roads at the start from Newport.

Links or other nearby trails: The **Newport to Pontypool Canal** shares the same start. There is a railway path starting just to the west of Crosskeys in the

Sirhowy Valley Country Park. The **Taff Trail** runs north from Cardiff.

 Map + Leaflet: OS Landranger Map 171.

 Refreshments: In Newport, Risca and Crosskeys, just off the canal.

Nearest Railway: Newport.

164. NEWPORT TO PONTYPOOL CANAL, South Wales

This is the second of two canals running north from Newport. Sections have been built over, particularly through Cwmbran. However, as with the Cross Keys Canal, it is a surprisingly green corridor through such an urban area.

 The route: Newport (Barrack Hill) – Cwmbran – Pontypool.

Distance: 9 miles one way, 18 miles both.

Category: Canal towpath.

Start + Parking: Malpas Road (A4042), Newport. From M4 Jct 26 take the A4042 south towards Newport then park in one of the side streets to the right (Goodrich Crescent, Ross Lane, Walford Street). To get to the canal, follow Malpas Road for 200 yards south as far as the pedestrian bridge over the road. At this point turn right and keep bearing right to join the start of the canal towpath. Pass beneath a bridge then shortly you have a choice. At the next new stone bridge turn right beneath the M4 for Pontypool or continue straight ahead for Cross Keys.

 Surface + Hills: Stone and gravel path. Gradual climb from Newport to Pontypool.

Roads + Road crossings: Short road section at the start to get to the canal. There is

a 0.75 mile section in Cwmbran where the canal has been built over. If you follow the pavement parallel with the A4051 you will rejoin the canal.

Links or other nearby trails: The **Newport to Cross Keys Canal** shares the same start. There is a railway path in the **Sirhowy Valley Country Park**, to the west of Cross Keys. There are plans to link the canal to the **Pontypool to Blaenavon** railway path.

 Map + Leaflet: OS Landranger Map 171.

 Refreshments: In Newport, Cwmbran and Pontypool, just off the route.

Nearest Railway: Newport, Cwmbran and Pontypool.

Routes in Northern Ireland

THE LAGAN TOWPATH, Stranmillis to Lisburn, County Antrim.
A medium distance linear route of 13 miles within the Lagan Valley Regional Park. This trail can be cycled in either direction.

 The route: Way marked towpath route that forms part of the Ulster Way. Distance: 13 miles.

Category: Riverside towpath.

Start + Parking: There is a car park close to the Stranmillis Boat Club in Belfast. To get there take the Stranmillis Road to the Stranmillis Roundabout at the bottom of the hill. Take the exit towards the boat club which is on Lough View Road .

 Surface + Hills: Totally flat high quality bitmac surface for the entire distance.

Roads and road crossings: There is one minor B road to be crossed close to Hilden.

 Maps and Leaflets: OS Northern Ireland Discovery Series Map 20.

 Refreshments: Lots of choice on the Stranmillis Road and in Lisburn.

Nearest railway: Botanic or Lisburn.

BALLYPATRICK FOREST PARK near
Ballycastle, North Antrim
A spectacular circular forest route that can be extended if you venture into any one of the network of navigable paths off the main loop. Cars are allowed entrance into the forest but the speed limit is set at 20 mph. The density of cars is low. The extensive network of alternative

aths mentioned above are totally traffic free. Cyclists do not pay the admission fee charged to drivers.

 The route: A one way circuitous forest path starting from the car park. Alternatively get side-tracked on the traffic free trails.

Distance: 5.5 miles or longer.

Category: Woodland trail

Start + Parking: The forest park is situated between Ballycastle and Cushendall along the A2. The entrance and car park is 5 miles from Ballycastle and roughly 16 miles from Cushendall, it is signposted in both directions.

 Surface + Hills: The main route is partly high quality bitmac surface turning to gravel track.

Roads and road crossings: The A2 must be used for 0.5 mile to return to the start.

Links to other nearby trails: The Giant's Causeway to Bushmills trail is 18 miles west of Ballycastle.

 Maps and Leaflets: OS Northern Ireland Discovery Series Map 5.

 Refreshments: Lots of choice in Ballycastle and Cushendall.

Nearest Railway: Nothing really close.

CITY PARKS AND CRAIGAVON LAKES, County Armagh

This is first section of the National Cycling Network to be opened in Northern Ireland and offers cyclists totally traffic free cycling paths set in hundreds of acres of woodland, wetlands and meadows. The surrounding built up areas of Portadown, Brownlow and Lurgan are accessed via a series of linking paths.

 The route: A way marked linear route that can be extended around the Craigavon City Park and its lakes.

Distance: 6 miles or longer if desired.

Category: Mixed terrain incorporating wetlands, open meadows and woodland.

Start + Parking: Car parking at the Lough Neagh Discovery Centre at Oxford Island. Take the M1 to junction 10.

 Surface + Hills: Flat high quality bitmac paths and gravel tracks.

Roads and road crossings: A short section of minor road is used and other minor roads have to be crossed.

Links to other nearby trails: None to date, there are however plans to link up Portadown and Moira via Aghalee and Broadwater.

 Maps and Leaflets: OS NI Map 20. And the Craigavon leaflet available from Sustrans in Belfast, tel: 02890 434569

 Refreshments: There is a tea room at the Discovery Centre there is also plenty of choice in Craigavon Centre and in

Portadown.

Nearest Railway: Lurgan Station is 2.5 miles from the Discovery Centre.

GIANT'S CAUSEWAY TO BUSHMILLS

A short route of only five miles round-trip that passes the wilderness and loneliness of Bushfoot Strand. This is a delightful coastal path that takes you close to the world's oldest whiskey distillery at Bushmills. Tours are available.

 The route: Way marked North Atlantic Coastal route.

Distance: 5 miles round-trip.

Category: Coastal trail

Start + Parking: Car park at the Giant's Causeway Visitors Centre. This is found along the B146 which is a loop road off the A2 between the towns of Ballycastle and Bushmills.

 Surface & Hills: Relatively flat compacted dirt trail.

Roads + road crossings: A very short section of minor road is used.

Links to other nearby trails: Ballypatrick Forest Park is about 5 miles from Ballycastle along the A2 going towards Cushendall.

 Maps and Leaflets: OS NI Discovery Series Maps 4 or 5.

 Refreshments: The Distillery; National Tea Room; or the Causeway Hotel.

Nearest Railway: Portrait, 12 miles east of The Causeway.

165. NICKY LINE, from Hemel Hempstead to Harpenden

One of four short rides along railway paths in Hertfordshire. The name may have come from 'funicular' referring to the steep gradients along the line.

 The route: Hemel Hempstead (Eastman Way Trading Estate) – B487 / A5185 roundabout – Harpenden (Park Hill).

Distance: 5 miles one way, 10 miles both.

Category: Railway path.

Start + Parking: Park Hill, Harpenden. Take the A1081 Luton Road then turn left immediately after going under the railway bridge. Also at Eastman Way Trading Estate, Hemel Hempstead (off the B487).

 Surface + Hills: Fine gravel path. Gentle climb SW from Harpenden.

Roads + Road crossings: Three busy roads to cross – the B487 (twice) and the A5183. **Take great care.**

Links or other nearby trails: The **Grand Union Canal** passes through Hemel Hempstead.

 Map + Leaflet: OS Landranger Map 166.

 Refreshments: Lots of choice in Harpenden.

Nearest Railway: Harpenden.

166. NORTH DOWNS WAY, Surrey and Kent

Unlike the **South Downs Way**, or the **Ridgeway**, where you are allowed to cycle from one end to the other, the North Downs Way, running along the chalk ridge from Farnham to Canterbury and Dover, is mainly a footpath and you are **not** permitted to cycle on footpaths. There are, however, several bridleway/byway sections that are open to cyclists. There are many good bases from which to explore the North Downs bridleway/byway network: Dorking, Peaslake, Walton on the Hill, Limpsfield and Wye. Tanners Hatch and Holmbury St Mary both have YHAs.

Bridleway/byway sections:
These stretches are almost all on bridleway, byway or minor road. If you take the appropriate Ordnance Survey Landranger maps you will be able to work out the best route for yourself.

1. Puttenham (west of Guildford) – Guildford – Dorking (OS maps 186 / 187)

2. Wrotham (M20 Jct 2) – Rochester – Blue Bell Hill (OS maps 178 / 188)

3. Hollingbourne (east of Maidstone) to Dunn Street (north of Ashford) (OS maps 188 / 189)

4. Canterbury to Dover (OS map 179)

 Surface + Hills: There are lots of hills and the surface can vary enormously, from a quiet tarmac lane or a fine stone path to a rough, muddy track, particularly in winter. Explore the area nearest to you on fine summer's day when most bridleways/byways will be rideable.

Roads + Road crossings: Several road crossings. Some road sections (on quiet minor lanes).

Map + Leaflet: OS Landranger Maps 178, 179, 186, 187, 188 +189.

167 – 188 NORTH EAST SCOTLAND FORESTRY COMMISSION – 22 routes

The area covered here is roughly bounded by a line drawn from Inverness to Aberdeen. See also North Scotland Forestry Commission.

Colour	Distance	Grade	Starting point
A. BUNZEACH (STRATHDON), *40 miles west of Aberdeen (near junction of A944 / A939)*			
167. Green	4 miles	Easy	Bellabeg Village Car Park /
168. Blue	5 miles	Easy	Semeil Car Park, near Strathdon
169. Red	8 miles	Moderate	
B. PITFICHIE, *16 miles west of Aberdeen, near junction of B993 / A944 (Monymusk)*			
170. Blue	9 miles	Moderate	Pitfichie Car Park,
171. Red	4 miles	Hard	southwest of Monymusk
C. GARTLY MOOR, *6 miles southwest of Huntly, off the A96 Aberdeen – Elgin road*			
172. Blue	3 miles	Moderate	Gartly Moor Car Park, on the
173. Red	5 miles	Moderate	minor road south of the A96
174. Brown	6 miles	Easy	towards Insch
D. KIRKHILL, *6 miles west of Aberdeen on the A96, at the junction with the B979*			
175. Red	5 miles	Moderate	Mountjoy Car Park
E. DURRIS, *15 miles southwest of Aberdeen, on the A957 south of junction with A93*			
176. White	8 miles	Moderate	Inchloan Car Park, on the minor road towards Inchloan, off the A957
177. Red	1 mile	Hard	Slug Road Car Park, on A957
F. BLACKHALL, *16 miles west of Aberdeen on the A93, just west of Banchory*			
178. White	5.5 miles	Easy	Shooting Greens Car Park, on the minor road between Potarch (A93, west of Banchory) and Waulkmill (B796, west of Strachan)
179. Red	7 miles	Easy	Banchory, on A93 west of Aberdeen
G. DRUMTOCHY, *25 miles southwest of Aberdeen, on the minor road between the B794 (Banchory – Montrose) and the village of Auchenblae*			
180. White	12.4 miles	Moderate	Drumtochty Glen Car Park, as above
H. FETTERESSO, *16 miles southwest of Aberdeen, on the A957 northwest of Stonehaven*			
181. Blue	9.3 miles	Easy	Swanley Car Park, on the minor road between Kirktown of Fetteresso and the A957
182. Yellow	6.8 miles	Easy	Slug Road Car Park, on the A957
183. Red	5.5 miles	Moderate	Quithel Car Park, on the minor road southwest of Kirktown of Fetteresso (Stonehaven)

J. WHITEASH & ORDIEQUISH, *10 miles east of Elgin, on the A96 south of Fochabers*

184. Orange	7.7 miles	Moderate	Winding Walks Car Park, 1 mile south of Fochabers on the A96
185. Blue	6.2 miles	Moderate	As above
186. Red	5.5 miles	Moderate	Slorach's Wood Car Park, on the minor road south from Fochabers parallel with the River Spey

K. BEN AIGAN, *12 miles southeast of Elgin, on the A95 southwest of Mulben*

187. Red	4.5 miles	Moderate	Ben Aigan Car Park (see above)
188. Blue	6 miles	Moderate	As above

Surface + Hills: Forestry tracks. The grading will give you an idea of the hills you may expect.

Map + Leaflet: OS Landranger Maps 28, 29, 30, 37, 38, 44 + 45. More useful is the leaflet produced by the Forestry Commission: *Cycling in the Forest – North East Scotland.* available from Forest Enterprise, North Scotland, 21 Church Street, Inverness. IV1 1EL. Tel: 01463 232811.

189 – 198 NORTH SCOTLAND FORESTRY COMMISSION – 10 ROUTES
This region lies to the north of a line drawn between Inverness and Ullapool.

Distance	**Markers**	**Grade**	**Starting point**

See also **North East Scotland Forestry Commission.**
A. TORRACHILTY, *20 miles northwest of Inverness, on the A835 north of Garve*
189. Glen Sgiach

16miles (one way)	Blue	Moderate	Contin Car Park

B. TRUDERSCRAIG, *35 miles southwest of Thurso, at the junction of the B871 & B873*
190. Trudesrcraig

13miles (one way)	Red	Moderate	Rosal Village Car Park

C. BORGIE, *30 miles west of Thurso on the A836, west of the junction with the B871*
191. Borgie Forest

9 miles (one way)	Blue	Moderate	Car park on A836

D. ARDROSS, *35 miles north of Inverness, off the A9 to the west of Tain*
192. Morangie Hill

14 miles	Green	Moderate	Lamington Car park on minor road southwest of Tain

193. Strathrory

22 miles	Purple	Hard	

E. BLACK ISLE, *10 miles north of Inverness, on the minor road parallel with the A832 (next to the Mount Eagle Mast on the Munlochy to Culbokie Road)*
194. Military Road

10 miles	Red	Moderate	As above

F. CAMSTER, *12 miles southwest of Wick, on the minor road running north from the A99, starting just east of Lybster*

195. Camster Forest

14 miles	Red	Moderate	As above

G. LAEL, *7 miles south of Ullapool on the A835 near the village of Inverlael*

196. Upper Glen

8 miles	Red	Hard	As above

197. Riverside

4 miles	Purple	Easy	As above

H. ACHORMLARIE, *50 miles north of Inverness. Car park at Loch Buidhe on the minor road west of the A9, parallel and south of the A839.*

198. Beinn Donuill

8 miles	Green	Moderate	As above (one way)

 Surface + Hills: Forestry tracks. Lots of hills.

Roads + Road crossings: Some sections are on minor roads

 Map + Leaflet: OS Landranger Maps 10, 11, 16, 17, 19, 20, 21 + 26. Much better is the leaflet produced by the Forestry Commission – *Cycling in the Forest – North Scotland* available from Forest Enterprise, North Scotland, 21 Church Street, Inverness. IV1 1EL. Tel: 01463 232811.

---

199. NORTH TYNE CYCLEWAY
(Hadrian's Way), Newcastle

There are traffic-free trails along both sides of the Tyne east from Wylam. The North Tyne Cycleway runs from Wylam to The Quayside in the heart of Newcastle upon Tyne and will eventually run all the way to Tynemouth along the course of Hadrian's Wall Path National Trail.

 The route: Wylam – Newburn – Scotswood – Newcastle Quayside (the Swing Bridge).

Distance: 9 miles one way, 18 miles both.

Category: Railway path.

Start + Parking: Wylam, Newburn Leisure Centre or Newcastle Quayside (the Swing Bridge).

 Surface + Hills: Tarmac / gravel path. No hills.

Roads + Road crossings: No dangerous crossings.

Links or other nearby trails: South of the Tyne, the **Keelman's Way** runs from Wylam to Hebburn Riverside Park (west of Jarrow). A short section of the North Tyne Cycleway is used on Sustrans **C2C** Route which crosses the country from the Cumbrian Coast at Whitehaven (or Workington) to the East Coast at Tynemouth or Sunderland.

Cycle Hire: Newcastle Cycle Centre, 165 Westgate Road, Newcastle upon Tyne. Tel: 0191 222 1695.

 Map + Leaflet: OS Landranger Map 88. Hadrian's Way leaflet

---

available from Planning Dept, City of Newcastle upon Tyne, Civic Centre, Barras Bridge, Newcastle upon Tyne. NE1 8PH. Tel: 0191 232 8520.

 Refreshments: All along the way.

Nearest Railway: Wylam, Newcastle.

200. NUTBROOK TRAIL, west of Nottingham
A dismantled railway that forms part of Sustrans Millennium Route, there are plans to extend the route in both directions linking with Derby, Nottingham, Chesterfield and the Trans Pennine Trail.

 The route: Long Eaton – Sandiacre – Kirk Hallam.

Distance: 6 miles one way, 12 miles both.

Category: Railway path.

Start + Parking: Midland Street, Long Eaton (near the junction of the A6005 and the B6540, southwest of Nottingham). Parking near to the Council Offices. Or at Straws Bridge, Kirk Hallam (A6096 south of Ilkeston).

 Surface + Hills: Stone and gravel path. No hills.

Roads + Road crossings: No dangerous crossings.

Links or other nearby trails: Shipley Country Park lies 4 miles north of Kirk Hallam.

 Map + Leaflet: OS Landranger Map 129. Leaflet available from Erewash Borough Council. Tel: 0115 944 0440.

 Refreshments: Long Eaton, Sandiacre, Kirk Hallam.

Nearest Railway: Long Eaton.

OBAN – see 275 – 279. West of Scotland Forestry

201. OGMORE VALLEY, north of Bridgend, South Wales
A splendid example of what can be done with the old railway lines that used to bring coal down from the Welsh valleys to the coast now that the region finds itself in a post–coal mining era.

 The route: Brynmenyn (north of Bridgend) – Blackmill – Ogmore Vale – Nant y Moel.

Distance: 7 miles one way, 14 miles both.

Category: Railway path.

Start + Parking: The garage / pub / Post Office and stores in Blackmill, at the junction of the A4093 and A4061, 4 miles north of M4 Jct 36. Park just beyond the Fox & Hounds pub and garage. The path starts on the other side of the river. It runs 2 miles south to Brynmenyn or 5 miles north to Nantymoel.

 Surface + Hills: Stone and gravel path. Steady climb from south to north.

Roads + Road crossings: Minor roads to cross.

Links or other nearby trails: The Taff Trail runs from Cardiff to Brecon. There are waymarked trails from Afan Argoed Countryside Centre northeast of Port Talbot. The Rhondda Community forest routes start in Cwmparc, to the west of Treorchy (in the Rhondda valley).

Map + Leaflet: OS Landranger Map 170.

 Refreshments: In Blackmill, Ogmore Vale and Nant y moel.

Nearest Railway: Aberkenfig (north of Bridgend).

202. OXFORD CANAL
As with any long section of canal towpath you must be prepared for a mixture of all sorts of surfaces and allow plenty of time as you follow this meandering waterway north from Oxford to Banbury and beyond.

NB Please read *The Waterways Code – Cycling on the towpath* at the back of the book.

 The route: Oxford city centre (Hythe Bridge Street, near the railway station) – Kidlington – Lower Heyford – Banbury – Cropredy – Fenny Compton (Bridge 136), just off the A423 north of Banbury.

Distance: 38 miles one way, 76 miles both.

Category: Canal towpath.

Start + Parking: The towpath starts on Hythe Bridge Street in the centre of Oxford. If arriving by car it would be better to start outside Oxford at one of the other places mentioned in **The Route**, above.

 Surface + Hills: Variable. From good stone track to a narrow, rutted path, muddy in winter and after rain. No hills.

Roads + Road crossings: No dangerous crossings.

Links or other nearby trails: The

Ridgeway is a long distance bridleway/ byway running from West Kennett to Goring on Thames.

 Map + Leaflet: OS Landranger Maps 164 + 151. You may prefer to use *Nicholson's Guide to the Waterways (South)* which is packed with extra information.

 Refreshments: All along the way.

Nearest Railway: Oxford, Tackley, Heyford, Kings Sutton and Banbury.

203. PEDDARS WAY, Norfolk
A long distance trail, suitable for mountain bikes, largely following the course of an old Roman Road which crosses the northern half of East Anglia from near Thetford to the Norfolk Coast at Holme next the Sea.

 The route: A11 northeast of Thetford – South Pickenham – Castle Acre – Fring – Ringstead – Holme next the Sea.

Distance: 53 miles one way, 106 miles both.

Category: Long distance trail.

Start + Parking: The trail starts 5 miles northeast of Thetford, on a layby just off the A11 Norwich road marked Peddars Way. This is hard to find! It is better to start at one of the many villages along the way. Castle Acre makes a very good base to explore the Peddars Way both north and south.

 Surface + Hills: Complete mixture – from tarmac lanes to good broad stone tracks to narrower grassy tracks which will be hard going in winter or after prolonged rain. Several gentle hills.

Roads + Road crossings: Several sections of lanes are used, including two short sections of 'B' roads. There are six 'A' roads to cross.

Links or other nearby trails: There are two waymarked trails in **Thetford Forest.**

 Map + Leaflet: OS Landranger Maps 132 + 144.

 Refreshments: At most of the villages.

Nearest Railway: Thetford or King's Lynn.

204. PENCAITLAND RAILWAY WALK, east of Edinburgh

One of several railway paths lying to the south and east of Edinburgh, the Pencaitland Railway Walk runs across predominantly arable land where there were once opencast coal mines.

 The route: West Saltoun – Pencaitland – Ormiston – Crossgatehall.

Distance: 6 miles one way, 12 miles both.

Category: Railway path.

Start + Parking: Car park in Pencaitland, just off the A6093 between Haddington and Dalkieth.

 Surface + Hills: Stone and gravel path. No hills.

Roads + Road crossings: the A6093 is crossed once.

Links or other nearby trails: The **Dalkieth to Penicuik Trail** starts 3 miles to the west of the end of the Pencaitland Walk. There is another railway path between **Haddington and Longniddry.**

 Map + Leaflet: OS Landranger Map 66. The *SPOKES Edinburgh Cycle Map* shows all the cycle routes in and around Edinburgh. Costs £3 available from SPOKES, The Lothian Cycle Campaign, St Martin's Church, 232 Dalry Road, Edinburgh. EH11 2JG. Tel: 0131 313 2114.

 Refreshments: None on the route.

Nearest Railway: Prestonpans.

205. PENDLE CYCLEWAYS from Colne to Brierfield, Lancashire

Three canals were built to cross the Pennines between Liverpool and Hull: the Huddersfield Narrow and Rochdale Canals took more direct lines whereas the Leeds & Liverpool, used in this route, made the most of the gap created by the tributaries of the Rivers Aire and Calder, reaching its highest point just north of Colne. Think about those poor navvies 200 years ago as you cycle along the towpath!

 The route: Colne – Leeds & Liverpool Canal – Brierfield.

Distance: 5 miles one way, 10 miles both.

Category: Canal towpath.

Start + Parking: Greenfield Road, Colne, at the northern end of the M65 to the north of Burnley. Follow Greenfield Road across a crossroads with Whitewalls Drive to Barrowford Locks and bear left along the towpath.

 Surface + Hills: Stone and gravel path. No hills.

Roads + Road crossings: Quiet residential roads are used at the start in Colne.

 Map + Leaflet: OS Landranger Map 103.

 Refreshments: In Colne, Nelson and Brierfield.

Nearest Railway: Colne, Nelson and Brierfield.

PEMBREY COUNTRY PARK, Llanelli, see **Wales (short routes).**

205a. PETERBOROUGH MILLENNIUM GREEN WHEEL, Cambridgeshire

The Peterborough Green Wheel is a network of cycleways, shared-use footpaths and bridleways that provide safe, continuous routes around the city and 'spokes' linking the Wheel to residential area and the city centre. Phase 1, opened in June 1998, runs through gently rolling hills, picturesque villages and open parkland to the west of the city. Phase 2 opened in September 1999 and runs from the waterfowl park at Peakirk through the open skies of the fens to the Bronze Age excavations of Flag Fen and along the River Nene to the city centre. The last link, to the south of the city, will be opened in September 2000.

 The route:
Phase 1: Ferry Meadows – Marholm – Bretton – Ferry Meadows (6 miles)
Ferry Meadows – Marholm – Etton – Glinton – Marholm – Bretton – Ferry Meadows (18 miles)
Phase 2: Peterborough Embankment – Flag Fen – Eye – Newborough – Borough Fen – Peakirk (22 miles)

Category: Bridleways and minor roads

Start + Parking:
Phase 1: Ferry Meadows Country Park, Oundle Road, Peterborough
Phase 2: City centre car parks close to the Embankment.

 Surface + Hills: Tarmac & gravel, very few hills.

Roads + Road crossings: Several crossings of minor roads. Take care crossing the old A15 north of Glinton. Stepped crossing at Hurn Road Bridge.

Links or other nearby trails: Connects with the west-east Sustrans route at Nene Park and Whittlesey and the north-south Sustrans route at Crowland and Yaxley.

 Map + Leaflet: OS Landranger Map 142. Leaflet maps available from Tourist Information Centre, Peterborough, tel: 01733 452336 or Peterborough Environment City Trust, tel: 01733 760883.

 Refreshments: Ferry Meadows Country Park; Waterfowl World, Peakirk; Flag Fen Visitor Centre; plus a choice of many village pubs en route.

Nearest Railway: Peterborough.

206. PLEASLEY TRAILS, northwest of Mansfield

The Pleasley Trails are three separate railway paths lying between Pleasley, Skegby and Teversal. They are linked together to form a circular route. Deep cuttings show the exposed limestone rock of the area.

 The route: Pleasley – Skegby – Teversal – Pleasley.

Distance: 5 miles.

Category: Railway paths.

Start + Parking:
1. Pit Lane, Pleasley, just off the A617 north-west of Mansfield. At the roundabout on the A617 in Pleasley take the exit signposted 'Pleasley, Teversal' then turn first right on to Pit Lane. Park here.

2. The Teversal Trail car park in Skegby, on Buttery Lane, just off the B6014 Mansfield to Tibshelf Road, signposted 'Manor Estate'.

 Surface + Hills: Narrow, stone–based track. No hills.

Roads + Road crossings: None.

Links or other nearby trails: The **Five Pits Trail** lies 5 miles to the west. **Clipstone Forest** lies 7 miles to the east.

 Map + Leaflet: OS Landranger Map 120.

 Refreshments: Carnarvon Arms, Fackley, just off the route, near Teversal.

Nearest Railway: Alfreton, to the south-west.

207. PLYM VALLEY TRAIL,
Plymouth, South Devon
This popular railway path climbs steadily as it runs north from Plymouth over a series of spectacular stone viaducts through the Plym valley towards Dartmoor.

 The route: Laira Bridge – Goodameavy.

Distance: 9 miles one way, 18 miles both.
Category: Railway path.

Start + Parking: The ride starts at Laira Bridge, Plymouth (where the A379 crosses the River Plym). There are car parks at Point Cottage, at the entrance to Saltram House grounds, at Plym Bridge and at Clearbrook.

 Surface + Hills: Stone and gravel path. Steady climb northwards.

Roads + Road crossings: Short road section through Bickleigh.

Links or other nearby trails: A trail runs along the old mineral tramway from **Princetown.**

 Map + Leaflet: OS Landranger Map 201.

 Refreshments: Pub in Clearbrook.

Nearest Railway: Plymouth.

208. PONTYPOOL TO BLAENAVON,
South Wales
This is part of Sustrans grand vision in South Wales which will create a route from Newport to Brynmawr to link via the Clydach Valley to Abergavenny and the Welsh National Route. Work is going on at the moment so the full route will be finished in the next year or so.

 The route:
1. Aberysychan north to Blaenavon.
2. Abersychan south to Pontypool and Cwmbran.

Distance:
5 miles north from Abersychan to Blaenavon, 10 miles return. 7 miles south from Abersychan to the Newport Canal in Cwmbran, 14 miles return.

Category: Railway path.

Start + Parking: The trail at present is at its most complete in Abersychan, north of Pontypool. It will be improved along its whole length in the near future. Start from the car park on The Promenade, Abersychan. To get there, from the centre of Abersychan, climb steeply on the B4246 (Union Street) signposted 'Tal y Waun, Garndiffaith'. On a sharp right hand bend after 3/4 mile with a railway arch ahead turn left sharply back on yourself onto The Promenade. Small car park after 400 yards, on a sharp right hand bend. Uphill for Blaenavon, downhill for Pontypool.

 Surface + Hills: Stone and gravel path. The path climbs steadily as it heads north from Cwmbran to Blaenavon.

Roads + Road crossings: Some roads are used through Pontypool.

Links or other nearby trails: The **Newport to Pontypool Canal** links with this trail. The **Newport to Crosskeys Canal** is in the next valley to the west.

 Map + Leaflet: OS Landranger Maps 161+ 171.

 Refreshments: Several pubs and cafes just off the route.

Nearest Railway: Pontypool.

PORTREATH TRAMROAD – see 214. Redruth & Chacewater Railway

209. PRINCETOWN, Dartmoor, Devon
A remote stretch of dismantled railway (formerly part of the Yelverton to Princetown line) in the heart of Dartmoor, starting from near the infamous Dartmoor Prison.

Distance: 6 miles one way, 12 miles round trip. It is suggested that you go as far as the first stile, before reaching the B3212.

Category: Railway path.

Start + Parking: The ride starts by the Fire Station in Princetown in the middle of

Dartmoor, signposted 'Disused Railway'. There is a pay and display car park in Princetown.

 Surface + Hills: Stone / gravel path. The trail drops almost 600 ft from Princetown to the B3212.

Roads + Road crossings: None.

Links or other nearby trails: The **Plym Valley Trail** from Plymouth.

Cycle Hire:
Family Cycle Hire, Peak Hill Farm, Yelverton.
01822 852908.
Tavistock Cycles Tel: 01822 617630.

 Map + Leaflet: OS Outdoor Leisure Map 28 (or three Landranger maps – 191, 201, 202).

 Refreshments: Several options in Princetown.

Nearest Railway: Nowhere nearby.

210. PRIORY COUNTRY PARK AND WILLINGTON COUNTRYWAY, Bedford
A short circuit of the lake in the country park plus a trip along the Willington Countryway railway path through woodland and arable land.

 The route: Priory Country Park, Bedford (off the A428 St Neots Road) – circuit of lake – Willington – minor road south of Great Barford.

Distance: 1.5 miles around the lake plus 4 miles one way along the Willington Countryway (ie 8 mile round trip).

Category: Lakeside route plus railway path.

Start + Parking: Priory Country Park,

Bedford signposted off the A428 St Neots Road.

 Surface + Hills: Fine gravel path. Short grassy section on the south side of the lake. No hills.

Roads + Road crossings: None, unless you wish to visit the pub and/or the Dovecote in Willington.

Links or other nearby trails: Grafham Water lies 15 miles to the north.

 Map + Leaflet: OS Landranger Map 153.

 Refreshments: Priory Marina pub at the start. The Crown pub in Willington.

Nearest Railway: Bedford.

211. QUANTOCKS RIDGE, Somerset

This is neither a waymarked railway path nor a forestry route, it's a bridleway that stays at close to 1000ft along its whole length. This is not a ride for young children.

 The route: The car park at West Bagborough – Triscombe Stone – Crowcombe Park Gate – Bicknoller Post – Beacon Hill.

Distance: 7 miles one way, 14 miles return.

Category: Bridleway ride along fine ridge.

Start + Parking: At the car park on the ridge to the east of West Bagborough. This is 10 miles east of Bridgwater on the road through Durleigh, Enmore and Timberscombe that crosses the Quantocks and drops down to Bishops Lydeard.

 Surface + Hills: Earth and stone track, muddy in winter. Several

hills, even though, essentially, you are on a ridge.

Roads + Road crossings: One minor road is crossed.

Links or other nearby trails: The **Bridgwater & Taunton Canal** lies to the southeast.

 Map + Leaflet: OS Landranger Map 181.

 Refreshments: Nothing on the ridge. There are pubs in most of the villages just below the ridge.

Nearest Railway: Taunton or Bridgwater.

212. QUEEN ELIZABETH COUNTRY PARK, Petersfield, Hampshire

Two routes have been waymarked in this popular country park at the western end of the South Downs. There is also a large Visitor Centre with a good cafe attached.

 Routes, distance, waymarkings, grade: Family trail 3.7 miles, purple waymarks, easy, some hills Mountain bike trail 3.2 miles, yellow waymarks, hard, with technical sections

Category: Forest trails.

Start + Parking: Queen Elizabeth Country Park, signposted off the A3, 4 miles south of Petersfield.

 Surface + Hills: Stone and gravel paths, forest tracks. Several hills.

Roads + Road crossings: None.

Links or other nearby trails: The **South Downs Way** passes through Queen Elizabeth Country Park.

Cycle Hire: Bike hire at the park. Tel: 01705 591018 or 0385 597364.

 Map + Leaflet: OS Landranger Map 197. Leaflet can be purchased from the Visitor Centre.

 Refreshments: At the Visitor Centre.

Nearest Railway: Petersfield.

213. QUEEN ELIZABETH FOREST PARK, Trossachs, north of Glasgow

The Forest Park covers three forests in the Aberfoyle/Callander area – Strathyre, Achray and Loch Ard – and there are several way-marked routes in each of the three holdings. They have been undergoing a radical overhaul so exact details cannot be given. The new routes and a new leaflet are expected soon.

Category: Forest trails.

Start + Parking:
1. Aberfoyle Tourist Information Centre (A81 north of Glasgow).
2. Queen Elizabeth Forest Park Visitor Centre, on the A821 north of Aberfoyle.
3. Strathyre Information Centre (A84 north of Callander)

 Surface + Hills: Forest tracks. Lots of hills!

Roads + Road crossings: Some sections of minor road are used.

Links or other nearby trails: The Sustrans Glasgow – Inverness National Cycle Network passes through Aberfoyle and Callander. There is a route alongside the north side of **Loch Katrine.**

Cycle Hire: Trossachs Cycle Hire, Trossachs Holiday Park, 3 miles south of Aberfoyle on A81. 01877 382614.

 Map + Leaflet: OS Landranger Map 57. A leaflet (£1) is produced by Forest Enterprise and is available from the Visitor Centres.

 Refreshments: In Aberfoyle, Callander and Strathyre.

Nearest Railway: Balloch, Milngavie or Dunblane.

214. REDRUTH & CHACEWATER RAILWAY PATH, Cornwall

There is a splendid, ongoing project to transform the old mineral tramways and railways of Cornwall to recreational use. It is suggested that you start from the Mineral Tramways Discovery Centre near Redruth and make up your own route. The network is well-signposted and there are many options to explore up to 30 miles of offroad tracks.

 The route: Several routes are possible from the Visitor Centre. The longest would head south, link with the Great Flat Lode Trail then go east along the old Redruth & Chacewater Railway through Twelveheads to Devoran.

Distance: There are over 30 miles of offroad trails made from converting old tramways and old railways. The network is well signposted and with the aid of a map (see details below) you will be able to design a route to suit you.

Category: Railway path, mineral tramways and quiet lanes.

Start + Parking: Mineral Tramways Discovery Centre, Old Cowlins Mill, Penhallick, Carn Brea, Redruth. Tel: 01209 613978. (Between Camborne and Redruth, south of the A3047 on the Pool – Four Lanes Road). It's closed on Saturdays.

The Family Cycling Trail Guide

Surface + Hills: Tarmac lanes, stone / gravel path, at times a bit rough. Several gentle climbs.

Roads + Road crossings: The road uses some sections of quiet roads.

Links or other nearby trails: This is an ongoing project and more miles of converted railways and tramways will be added each year to the network.

 Map + Leaflet: OS Landranger Maps 203 + 204. Much better is are the three leaflets produced by Kerrier District Councila and available from the Discovery Centre.

 Refreshments: Pubs in Devoran and Scorrier.

Nearest Railway: Perranwell Station.

215. RHONDDA COMMUNITY ROUTES, Treorchy, South Wales
South Wales has hundreds of square miles of forestry and in some cases there are waymarked trails, such as these up above the Rhondda Valley, once the greatest coal producing area in the world.

 The route: Cwm Parc (west of Treorchy) – forestry tracks west then north – A4061 at Mynydd Beili-glas, north of Treherbert.

Distance: 12 miles one way, 24 return.

Category: Forest trail.

Start + Parking: Cwmparc, west of Treorchy, off the A4061 Treorchy – Bridgend road. Alternatively start at the car park at the top of the pass on the A4061 north of Treherbert. The route is waymarked with red markers 'Rhondda Community Route'.

 Surface + Hills: Forest tracks.

One very steep climb up from Treorchy. Steady climb at the northern end of the route to the highpoint at Mynydd Beili–glas (almost 2000 ft!).

Roads + Road crossings: None. If you want to make the ride into a loop you could come back down the A4061.

Links or other nearby trails: There is a railway path in **Ogmore Vale**. There are several waymarked trails from **Afan Argoed Country Park**, northeast of Port Talbot.

 Map + Leaflet: OS Landranger Map 170. Leaflet available from Rhondda Borough Council, tel: 01443 680669 or Valleys Forest Initiative, tel: 01639 850564.

 Refreshments: In Treorchy.

Nearest Railway: Treorchy.

216. RICHMOND PARK, London
Created by the generosity of an anonymous donor who wanted the trail named after his daughter, Tamsin, this 8 mile purpose-built shared use path is one of the best things to have happened to recreational cycling in London.

 The route: A circuit of Richmond Park.

Distance: The Tamsin Trail around Richmond Park is 8 miles long.

Category: Cycle track around the park.

Start + Parking: Any of the car parks near the gates / entrances into Richmond Park.

 Surface + Hills: Fine gravel path. Several gentle hills.

Roads + Road crossings: Several roads are crossed in the park.

Links or other nearby trails: The Thames Towpath runs through Richmond.

 Map + Leaflet: OS Landranger Map 176. Park map available from Royal Parks, Richmond Park, Richmond, Surrey TW10 5HS. Tel 0208 948 3209.

 Refreshments: There is a cafe at Pembroke Lodge on the west side of the park, and near Roehampton Gate on the east side.

Nearest Railway: Richmond or Kingston.

217. RIDGEWAY AND ICKNIELD WAY

*The Ridgeway, like the **South Downs Way**, is a long distance trail open to cyclists along its entire length from West Kennett to Goring on Thames, northwest of Reading. From Goring northwest to Chinnor, it is known as both the Icknield Way and Ridgeway and is a mixture of footpath and bridle-way. It is a glorious, challenging route to be undertaken in summer, on mountain bikes.*

 The route: West Kennett (west of Marlborough on the A4) – Ogbourne St George – Uffington – Goring – Watlington –Chinnor.

Distance: 85 miles from West Kennett to Ivinghoe Beacon.

Category: Long distance trail.

Start + Parking: West Kennett, Ogbourne St George, Uffington Castle, Goring, Watlington, Chinnor.

 Surface + Hills: Stone–based track, sections are muddy in winter and after prolonged rain. Lots

of hills. Mountain bikes only.

Roads + Road crossings: Several road crossings and sections of quiet lanes.

Links or other nearby trails: The **Kennet & Avon Canal** lies 6 miles south of the start at West Kennett. The Ridgeway crosses the **Marlborough–Chiseldon Railway Path.**

 Map + Leaflet: OS Landranger Maps 165, 173, 174 + 175.

 Refreshments: It will be necessary to come off the ridge to find refreshments except at Ogbourne St George. Beyond Goring the trail is at a lower level and refreshments are closer by.

Nearest Railway: Pewsey, Didcot, Goring, Princes Risborough.

218. RISING SUN COUNTRY PARK, north of Newcastle upon Tyne

The ride follows the old Coxlodge Waggonway into the Rising Sun Country Park which has been created on the site of a former colliery.

 The route: South Gosforth (junction of the A191 / A189) – east through Little Benton Farm – Rising Sun Country Park.

Distance: 5 miles one way, 10 miles return.

Category: Railway path.

Start + Parking: The trail starts on the A191, just off the roundabout with the A189 in South Gosforth. Also at Rising Sun Countryside Centre.

Surface + Hills: Mixture of tarmac and gravel path. Mountain bikes recommended. No hills.

Roads + Road crossings: Two busy roads to cross – the A188 and A186. A short section of quiet lane is used near Rising Sun Farm.

Links or other nearby trails: The North Tyne Cycleway runs along the north bank of the Tyne. Keelman's Way runs along the south bank.

Cycle Hire:
1. Newcastle Cycle Centre, 265 Westgate Road, Newcastle. Tel: 0191 222 1695.
2. Rising Sun Countryside Centre. Tel: 0191 266 7733.

 Map + Leaflet: OS Landranger Map 88. Leaflet available from Environment and Strategy Team, North Tyneside Council. Tel: 0191 201 0033.

 Refreshments: Newton Park pub at Longbenton (A188). Light refreshments at the shop in the Rising Sun Countryside Centre.

Nearest Railway: Bikes cannot be carried on the Tyne & Wear Metro. The nearest railway is Newcastle, 3 miles to the south.

219. RIVER RAY PARKWAY, Swindon
This trail follows the course of the River Ray, crossing right through Swindon from northwest to southeast, linking two country parks – Coate Water and Mouldon Hill.

 The route: Coate Water Country Park (southeast Swindon) – Old Town – Mannington Recreation Ground – Mouldon Hill County Park.

Distance: 8 miles one way, 16 miles return.

Category: Railway path and riverside path.

Start + Parking: Coate Water Country Park, in the southeast corner of Swindon, off

the A4529, 2 miles northwest of M4, Jct 15.

 Surface + Hills: Stone and gravel path. No hills.

Roads + Road crossings: Several minor roads are crossed. Some quiet roads link the traffic-free sections.

Links or other nearby trails: The Marlborough – Chiseldon Path starts just south of Coate Water Country Park, the Cotswold Water Park lies to the northwest of Swindon. The Ridgeway is a long distance trail which runs from West Kennett to Goring on Thames.

 Map + Leaflet: OS Landranger Map 173. Leaflet showing the River Ray Parkway available from Great Western Community Forest, Swindon Borough Council, Premier House, Station Road, Swindon, Wiltshire. SN1 1TZ. Tel: 01793 466324.

 Refreshments: Several pubs just off the route.

Nearest Railway: Swindon.

220. RUDYARD LAKE,
near Leek, Staffordshire
A delightful ride alongside Rudyard lake with colourful yachts and dinghies set against a background of steep wooded slopes.

 The route: Rushton Spencer (off the A523 south of Macclesfield) – east side of Rudyard Lake – Leek.

Distance: 4.5 miles one way, 9 miles return.

Category: Railway path.

Start + Parking:
1. Car park near the Knot Inn at Rushton Spencer, just off the A523, 8 miles south of Macclesfield.

2. Also at the southern end of Rudyard Lake – turn off the A523, 2 miles northwest of Leek onto the B5331, signposted 'Rudyard Lake'. Just after going under a railway bridge turn left into the car park.

3. (Starting from Leek). Turn off A523 Macclesfield Road opposite Supersports Manufacturing on to the road next to Dyers Arms pub. The tarmac lane becomes a track. Join the railway path at the bridge.

 Surface + Hills: Stone–based track. Some muddy stretches on the northern section. No hills.

Roads + Road crossings: None.

Links or other nearby trails: The Biddulph Valley Trail lies 5 miles to the west. The Manifold Way starts at Waterhouses, on the A523, 8 miles south-east of Leek.

 Map + Leaflet: OS Landranger Map 118.

 Refreshments: Knot Inn pub in Rushton Spencer.

Nearest Railway: Congleton.

221. RUTLAND WATER,
east of Leicester
Britain's favourite reservoir route offering a superb day out around the largest man-made lake in Western Europe, covering an area of 3100 acres.

 The route: Egleton (near Oakham) – Manton – Edith Weston – Whitwell – Upper Hambleton.

Distance: 17 miles for the circuit plus 6 miles for the Hambleton Peninsula.

Category: Round reservoir route.

Start + Parking: Pay and display car parks at Normanton, Barnsdale, Whitwell and Empingham. Rutland Water lies between Oakham (A606 / A6003) and Stamford (A1).

 Surface + Hills: Good all year round track, at times tarmac. No major hills.

Roads + Road crossings: The section along the lane which leads from the A606 near Oakham to Hambleton Peninsula is fairly quiet, likewise the lane to Egleton. There is a busier 1 mile section east of Manton.

Other nearby trails: The Brampton Valley Way (between Market Harborough and Northampton) lies 16 miles to the southwest.

Cycle Hire: At Whitwell, tel: 01780 460705 or Normanton, tel: 01780 720888.

 Map + Leaflet: OS Landranger Map 141. The cycle hire outlets also have maps.

 Refreshments: Pubs in Edith Weston, Empingham, Whitwell, Hambleton and Manton.

Nearest Railway: Oakham.

SAINT HELEN'S CANAL
see **Sankey Valley Park**

SALE WATER PARK see **Mersey River through South Manchester**

222. SALFORD LOOPLINES,
west Manchester
The old railway line skirts Worsley Woods and offers the opportunity to visit the famous Worsley Canal Basin on the Bridgewater Canal.

The route: Little Hulton (Walkden, south of Bolton) – Worsley – Monton (west of Salford).

Distance: 5 miles one way, 10 miles return.

Category: Railway path.

Start + Parking: Monton Green (east of M63, Jct 1), Walkden (west of M62, Jct 14) or Little Hulton (southeast of M61, Jct 4). Car park in Monton Green at Duke's Drive Park just off Parrin Lane to the west of its junction with Monton Green (near Monton church).

Surface + Hills: Gravel and earth path. No hills.

Roads + Road crossings: Only minor road crossings.

Map + Leaflet: OS Landranger Map 109.

Refreshments: Pubs, cafes at Monton Green and Worsley Canal Basin.

Nearest Railway: Walkden Station. Cross the Walkden Road onto Park Road. At the junction by the bridge descend to the railway path via a gap stile in the fence.

223. SALT WAY, northwest of Stoke

A short, well–maintained stretch of dismantled railway through attractive woodland with a good family pub at the end of the ride.

The route: Hassall Green southeast to Alsager (northwest of Stoke).

Distance: 2.5 miles one way, 5 miles return.

Category: Railway path.

Start + Parking: Turn off the A533, 2.5 miles south of Sandbach (M6, Jct 17) opposite the New Inn pub onto New Inn Lane, signposted 'Hassall Green, Wheelock'. Go under the motorway and take the first right into the car park.

Surface + Hills: Good gravel path. No hills.

Roads + Road crossings: The B5078 is crossed at Lawton Heath End. If you decide to go to the pubs at either end of the trail there are short road sections.

Links or other nearby trails: The Biddulph Valley Trail is 5 miles east of Alsager. Rudyard Lake is 9 miles to the east.

Map + Leaflet: OS Landranger Map 118.

Refreshments: Lockside Cafe and Romping Donkey pub in Hassall Green or Wilbraham Arms 200 yards along the B5078 towards Alsager.

Nearest Railway: Alsager.

224. SANKEY VALLEY PARK & ST HELENS CANAL, Widnes, east of Liverpool

The trail runs from Sankey Bridge to Spike Island, along one of Britain's oldest canals to the shores of the Mersey near to Widnes.

Distance: 7.5 miles one way, 15 miles both.

Category: Canal towpath.

Start + Parking: Sankey Valley Park (near Bewsey Old Hall) on the west side of Warrington (A57 / A574), or the Catalyst Museum, Widnes (A533).

Surface + Hills: Tarmac, crushed gravel. Some rough sections on the canal towpath. No hills.

Roads + Road crossings: Take care at the busy crossing of the Liverpool Road at Sankey Bridges.

Links or other nearby trails: The **Warrington – Altrincham Trail** runs east from Warrington. The **Liverpool Loop Line** starts in Halewood, 5 miles west of Widnes.

 Map + Leaflet: OS Landranger Map 108.

 Refreshments: Bewsey Farm Inn near Old Hall. Ferry Tavern at Fiddlers Ferry. Cafe at Catalyst Museum.

Nearest Railway: Warrington Bank Quay.

225. SCARBOROUGH TO WHITBY RAILWAY PATH, North York Moors
The trail lies within the North York Moors National Park and follows a spectacular route along the North Yorkshire Heritage Coast.

 The route: Manor Road, Scarborough – Scalby – Cloughton – Ravenscar – Robin Hood's Bay – High Hawsker – southern edge of Whitby (near Larpool Hall).

Distance: 18 miles one way, 36 miles both.

Category: Railway path.

Start + Parking: Safeway car park in Scarborough (Manor Road, northwest of the town centre, near the cemetery). The trail can also be picked up in Scalby, Cloughton and Ravenscar and Robin Hood's Bay.

 Surface + Hills: Mixture of good and rough stone tracks. Mountain bikes recommended. Two climbs – one from Whitby to above Robin Hood's Bay (425 ft) and one from Scarborough to Ravenscar (625 ft).

Roads + Road crossings: Several minor road crossings and two busier roads (the A165 north of Scalby and the A171 near High Hawsker, south of Whitby). Several short sections on quiet roads through Robin Hood's Bay, Ravenscar and Scalby.

Links or other nearby trails: Waymarked forest trails in **Dalby Forest**, west of Scarborough.

Cycle Hire:
Bay Bike Hire, Glenray, Station Road, Robin Hood's Bay. Tel: 01947 880488.
North Rd Cycles, Whitby. Tel: 01947 820326.

 Map + Leaflet: OS Landranger Maps 94 + 101. A leaflet is also produced by Scarborough District Council. Tel: 01723 373333.

 Refreshments: Lots of choice in Scarborough, Robin Hood's Bay and Whitby. Cafe in Ravenscar.

Nearest Railway: Scarborough or Whitby.

226. SETT VALLEY TRAIL, Hayfield, southeast of Manchester
A short section of railway path on the western edge of the Peak District with fine views east towards Kinder Scout. It is worth visiting the New Mills Heritage Centre and the Torrs Riverside Park in New Mills.

 The route: Hayfield – New Mills. The trail ends at St George's Road where a sign indicates that there is no cycling beyond this point. If you

wish to go further you will either need to dismount and push your bikes through Riverside Park to The Torrs waterfalls (this will involve some steps) or go by road into New Mills (turn right on St Georges Road, right again at the T–junction at the bottom, cross the river then turn left into New Mills.

Distance: 3 miles one way, 6 miles return.

Category: Railway path.

Start + Parking: Sett Valley Visitor Centre in Hayfield. Turn off the A624 Glossop to Chapel-en-le-Frith road on to the A6015 to New Mills then first right on to Station Rd.

 Surface + Hills: Fine gravel path. No hills unless you go into New Mills.

Roads + Road crossings: No dangerous crossings. You will need to go on road if you

wish to visit New Mills.

Links or other nearby trails: The **Middlewood Way** (Marple to Macclesfield) lies west of New Mills. The **Longdendale Trail** starts at Padfield, north of Glossop.

Cycle Hire: At Hayfield Visitor Centre. Tel: 01663 746222.

 Map + Leaflet: OS Landranger Map 110. A leaflet is available from Hayfield Information Centre, Hayfield, Derbyshire. Tel: 01663 746222.

 Refreshments: Hot drinks at the Visitor Centre. Lots of choice in New Mills (this will involve a short road section).

Nearest Railway: New Mills.

SHARPNESS CANAL see 114.
Gloucester & Sharpness Canal

---

227. SHIPLEY COUNTRY PARK,
west of Nottingham

A country park near to Nottingham with several miles of quiet estate roads and good quality tracks around lakes and through woodland. Buy a map from the Visitor Centre and explore at leisure.

 Route and distance: Choose your own route through this cycle-friendly country park.

Category: Estate roads and tracks.

Start + Parking: The Information Centre at the entrance to Shipley Park, 1 mile south of Heanor (A6007). West of M1 Jct 26.

 Surface + Hills: Tarmac estate roads and stone-based tracks. Several gentle hills.

Roads + Road crossings: The roads in the Country Park carry light traffic.

Links or other nearby trails: There are several trails in and around Derby, 6 miles to the southwest.

Cycle Hire: At the Information Centre. Tel: 01773 719961.

 Map + Leaflet: OS Landranger Map 129. Better map available at the Information Centre.

 Refreshments: Cafe at the Information Centre.

Nearest Railway: Heanor.

228. SHROPSHIRE WOODLAND TRAILS, **southwest of Shrewsbury**

Two small Foresty Commission holdings in the beautiful countryside of Shropshire have way-marked routes through them. The routes can also be used for longer rides, using quiet lanes to link to nearby villages.
Routes, distance,

 waymarking, grade:
1. Bury Ditches, 3.5 miles (one way), waymarked, moderate
2. Eastridge Wood, 4 miles, Brown waymarks, easy
3. Eastridge Wood, 3 miles, Grey waymarks, hard
4. Eastridge Wood, 7 miles, Pink waymarks, moderate

Category: Forest trails

Start + Parking:
1. Bury Ditches Car Park. From Bishop's Castle (20 miles southwest of Shrewsbury on the A488) take the B4385 towards Lydbury North and Brockton. After 2 miles turn right onto a minor road through Brockton and Lower Down. You will shortly come to the Bury Ditches car park.

2. Poles Coppice car park. From the round-about in Minsterley (10 miles southwest of Shrewsbury on the A488) take the minor road eastwards towards Habberley. The car park is on the left, halfway up the hill.

 Surface + Hills: Forest roads. Several hills.

Roads + Road crossings: None in Bury Ditches. The routes through Eastridge Forest use minor roads.

 Map + Leaflet: OS Landranger Map 137 (Bury Ditches) and 126 (Eastridge Woods). Booklet called *Countryside & Woodland Cycle Trails* available from Shropshire Books, Winston Churchill Building, Radbrook Ctr, Shrewsbury. SY3 9BJ.

 Refreshments: Pub at Clunton, south of Bury Ditches. Pub in Habberley.

Nearest Railway: Church Stretton or Craven Arms.

229. SILKIN WAY, Telford, Shropshire

A fine trail along a green corridor right through the heart of this New Town, which nevertheless is full of reminders that this was the birthplace of the Industrial Revolution.

 The route: Coalport – Madeley – Hinkshay – Telford town centre – Trench – Hortonwood – Leegomery – Dothill – Bratton.

Distance: 14 miles one way, 28 miles return.

Category: Railway path.

Start + Parking: The China Museum, Coalport, on the road alongside the River Severn, parallel with the A442 to the south of Telford (south of M54 Jct 4).

 Surface + Hills: Tarmac or fine gravel path. Gentle climb up from Coalport.

Roads + Road crossings: Several road crossings, short sections of road are used, particularly on the section north from the town centre to Bratton.

Links or other nearby trails: There are three waymarked forest trails in **Cannock Chase** to the north of Cannock.

 Map + Leaflet: OS Landranger Map 127. A good booklet is produced by Leisure, Culture and Community Services, Telford & Wrekin Council, PO Box 211, Darby House, Telford TF3 4LA. Tel: 01952 202745.

 Refreshments: All along the way.

Nearest Railway: Telford or Wellington.

230. SIRHOWY COUNTRY PARK, northwest of Newport, South Wales

The valleys of South Wales are synonymous with coal mining. Now that the pits have all closed, more and more of the old railways that used to transport coal down to the docks are being converted to recreational use. Sirhowy Valley Country Park not only has a section of railway path but also some waymarked woodland trails.

 The route: The Sirhowy Valley Country Park Visitor Centre (west of Crosskeys) north along the valley of the Sirhowy River to Wyllie.

Distance: 5 miles one way, 10 miles return.

Category: Railway path.

Start + Parking: At the car park just off the roundabout at the junction of the A467 and A4048 to the west of Crosskeys (northwest of M4 Jct 28).

 Surface + Hills: Gravel path. Gentle climb up to Wyllie.

Roads + Road crossings: None.

Links or other nearby trails: The **Newport to Crosskeys Canal** lies 1 mile to the east.

 Map + Leaflet: OS Landranger Map 171. Leaflet available from the Visitor Centre.

 Refreshments: Pub in Wyllie.

Nearest Railway: Hengoed (Ystrad Mynach).

231. SLOUGH ARM, Grand Union Canal, east of Slough.

The towpath of the Grand Union Canal close to London is generally maintained to a very high standard. There are several 'arms' coming off the main canal: others are to be found at Wendover, Aylesbury and Northampton.

The route: Cowley Peachey Junction (south of Uxbridge) – Iver – Langley – Slough.

Distance: 5 miles one way, 10 miles return.

Category: Canal towpath.

Start + Parking: Cowley Peachey Junction lies 3 miles south of Uxbridge on the A408. (Just north of Yiewsley). The terminus is on the B416 Stoke Poges road to the north of Slough Railway Station.

 Surface + Hills: Gravel path. No hills.

Roads + Road crossings: None.

Links or other nearby trails: The Grand Union Canal itself, Windsor Great Park.

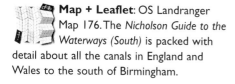 **Map + Leaflet**: OS Landranger Map 176. The *Nicholson Guide to the Waterways (South)* is packed with detail about all the canals in England and Wales to the south of Birmingham.

 Refreshments: Iver, Langley and Slough.

Nearest Railway: Yiewsley, Iver, Langley, Slough.

232. SNEATON FOREST, south of Whitby, North York Moors
Several new routes are planned for the near future in the North Riding Forest Park starting from the Low Dalby Visitor Centre. This long distance, cross-forest route has been left in place. From north to south it crosses Sneaton Forest, Langdale Forest and Dalby Forest. You will need a leaflet and map.

 The route: Falling Foss car park (B1416 south of Whitby) – Sneaton Forest – Langdale Forest – Dalby Forest – Thornton le Dale (A170 east of Pickering).

Distance: 18 miles one way, 36 miles return.

Category: Forest trail.

Start + Parking: Falling Foss car park off the B1416, 5 miles south of Whitby.

 Surface + Hills: Forestry tracks. Several steep hills.

Roads + Road crossings: The trail shares the course of the Forest Drive at its southern end. A minor road is used into Thornton le Dale.

Links or other nearby trails: There are other waymarked forest trails in Dalby Forest.

 Map + Leaflet: OS Landranger Maps 94 + 100. A large leaflet can be purchased from Forest Enterprise, North York Moors District, Outgang Road, Pickering. YO18 7EL. Tel: 01751 472771.

 Refreshments: At the Low Dalby Vistor Centre. Lots of choice in Thornton le Dale.

Nearest Railway: Norton.

233. SOUTH DOWNS WAY
A magnificent trail along the chalk downs that lie between the sea and the Vale of Sussex. In its entirety, this a tough challenge for mountain bikers; there are, however, several ridge sections along broad stone-based tracks which are appropriate for families on hybrid/mountain bikes to explore in the summer months. These

include Rackham Hill, south of Storrington, Chanctonbury Ring, west of Steyning, either side of Ditchling Beacon (north of Brighton) and west of Firle Beacon.

 The route: Winchester – Buriton (south of Petersfield) – Amberley (north of Arundel) – Chanctonbury Ring (west of Steyning) – Ditchling Beacon (north of Brighton) – Alfriston – Eastbourne.

Distance: 100 miles one way. The four ridge sections mentioned in the introduction are 3-7 miles long.

Category: Long distance trail, all bridleway status.

Start + Parking: If you are looking for a relatively flat section along a ridge, the trick is to start from a car park at the top of a hill! There are several of these (mentioned in the Introduction, above) which it would be too complicated to give directions for – use Ordnance Survey maps to find the most convenient one for you – map details below.

 Surface + Hills: From broad, stone–based tracks to grassy bridleways. Lots of hills. Mountain bikes only.

Roads + Road crossings: Several main roads to cross along the whole trail.

Links or other nearby trails: The whole of the South Downs are criss–crossd with bridleways, making it the best mountain biking area in the Southeast of England. There is a waymarked trail in **Friston Forest** and the **Downs Link** runs north from Steyning to Guildford. The **Cuckoo Trail** starts at Polegate, 2 miles north of Eastbourne.

Cycle Hire: Arundel Cycle Hire, 4 School Lane, Arundel, West Sussex. Tel: 01903 883712.

 Map + Leaflet: OS Landranger Maps 185, 197, 198, 199.

 Refreshments: Little on the ridge itself. With occasional exceptions, you will need to descend to the towns and villages beneath the downs to find pubs and cafes.

Nearest Railway: Winchester, Petersfield, Amberley, Lewes, Eastbourne.

SOUTH TYNE CYCLEWAY
see 136. Keelman's Way

234. SOUTHWELL TRAIl,
east of Mansfield, Nottinghamshire
You are in Robin Hood country around these parts and indeed the long distance footpath called the Robin Hood Way uses a section of this railway path that runs through the old coal mining area of Nottinghamshire.

 The route: Bilsthorpe (east of Mansfield) – Farnsfield – Southwell (west of Newark).

Distance: 8 miles one way, 16 miles return.

Category: Railway path.

Start + Parking:
1. At the roundabout at the southeast corner of Bilsthorpe, 2 miles northwest of the roundabout at the junction of the A617 and A614 east of Mansfield.

2. At the northeast corner of Southwell, on the minor road towards Hockerton (off the A612 to the west of Newark on Trent.

 Surface + Hills: Stone and gravel path. No hills.

Roads + Road crossings: Several minor and one major road to cross, the A617 south of Bilsthorpe.

Links or other nearby trails: There is a waymarked forest trail in **Clipstone Forest**.

 Map + Leaflet: OS Landranger Map 120.

 Refreshments: In Bilsthorpe, Farnsfield and Southwell.

Nearest Railway: Fiskerton Station, east of Southwell.

SOUTH WEST SCOTLAND FORESTRY – see 79 – 99.
Dumfries & Galloway

235. STAFFORD – NEWPORT GREENWAY, Staffordshire
A short ride on a dismantled railway to the west of Stafford, best seen in late spring or early summer when the wildflowers are at their best. There are plans to continue the section open to cyclists beyond the present finish towards Newport.

 The route: The new housing estate at Castlefields, west of Stafford – Derrington – car park on the minor road north of Haughton.

Distance: 3.5 miles one way, 7 miles both.

Category: Railway path.

Start + Parking: Take the A518 out of Stafford towards Telford. Turn off this road at the new housing estate at Castlefields. Follow Martin Drive from the first roundabout by Castlefields then go straight ahead at the second roundabout on to the narrow lane signposted 'No Through Road'. There is a car park along to the left. Exit the car park, turn left along the narrow lane then at the end of the factories on the right turn right to join the railway path.

 Surface + Hills: Stone and gravel track. No hills.

Roads + Road crossings: None.

Links or other nearby trails: The **Silkin Way** runs through Telford. There are plenty of forest tracks in **Cannock Chase** to the southeast of Stafford.

 Map + Leaflet: OS Landranger Map 127.

 Refreshments: The Red Lion pub, Derrington.

Nearest Railway: Stafford.

236. STAVELEY TO KILLAMARSH AND ROTHER VALLEY COUNTRY PARK, southeast of Sheffield
The trail follows the line of the former Great Central Railway. There are plans to extend the path through Rother Valley Country Park to Rotherham.

 The route: Staveley (near the junction of the A619 and B6053) southeast of Sheffield – Renishaw – Killamarsh – Rother Valley Country Park.

Distance: 6 miles one way, 12 miles return.

Category: Railway path.

Start + Parking: Rother Valley Country Park, accessed from the A618 to the south-east of Sheffield (between Killamarsh and Aston, southwest of M1 JCt 31). Or Staveley, on the A619 between Chesterfield and Worksop.

 Surface + Hills: Stone and gravel path. No hills.

Roads + Road crossings: None.

Links or other nearby trails: Clumber Park is just south of Worksop.

 Map + Leaflet: OS Landranger Map 120.

 Refreshments: Staveley, Renishaw, Killamarsh.

Nearest Railway: Woodhouse Mill, east of Sheffield.

237. STONEHOUSE – NAILSWORTH RAILWAY PATH, south of Gloucester

The Cotswolds grew prosperous in the Middle Ages with the wool trade and later developed cloth mills pre-dating the mills of Northern England by a century. The ride along the Stroud Valley passes many of the old mills and links two towns whose fortunes rose and fell with the trade.

 The route: Ryeford – Dudbridge – (southwest of Stroud) – Nailsworth.

Distance: 6 miles one way, 12 miles return.

Category: Railway path.

Start + Parking: Ryeford, on the A419 southeast of Stonehouse, 4 miles east of M5 Jct 13. Or Nailsworth, near the Railway Hotel.

 Surface + Hills: Stone and gravel path. Gentle climb from Stonehouse to Nailsworth.

Roads + Road crossings: Several minor roads to cross.

Links or other nearby trails: The Gloucester & Sharpness Canal starts at Sharpness, west of Stroud.

 Map + Leaflet: OS Landranger Map 162.

 Refreshments: Nailsworth.

Nearest Railway: Stonehouse.

238. STRATFORD GREENWAY, southwest of Straford upon Avon

Finding the start of the trail will be your hardest task if you choose to explore this railway path running southwest from Shakespeare's Stratford and crossing the River Avon on a fine metal bridge.

 The route: Stratford –upon–Avon to Long Marston.

Distance: 5 miles one way, 10 miles return.

Category: Railway path.

Start + Parking: It is very hard to give detailed instructions to get to the car park at the start! If you follow signs for the race course and the B439 to Bidford–on–Avon you will pick up signs for the Stratford Greenway.

 Surface + Hills: Good stone and gravel path. No hills.

Roads + Road crossings: One minor road to cross. Short section on a quiet road if you wish to visit the pub at Long Marston.

Links or other nearby trails: Stratford upon Avon Canal. Grand Union Canal.

 Map + Leaflet: OS Landranger Map 151.

 Refreshments: Masons Arms pub, Long Marston (just off the route).

Nearest Railway: Stratford.

239. STRATHBLANE – KIRKINTILLOCH (Strathkelvin Walkway), north of Glasgow

There are a plethora of traffic-free tracks in and around Glasgow, some use riverside paths, some use canal towpaths and others, like this trail, use dismantled railways. This is one of the most spectacular, running parallel with the dramatic Campsie Fells, which rise to almost 2000 ft on Earl's Seat, to the north of Strathblane.

 The route: Strathblane – Lennoxtown – Milton of Campsie – Kirkintilloch.

Distance: 8 miles one way, 16 miles return.

Category: Railway path.

Start + Parking: Strathblane, 10 miles north of Glasgow on the A81. The trail starts just to the east of the junction with the A891. Or start at Kirkintilloch, 8 miles northeast of Glasgow on the A803. The trail starts on the north side of town on the B757 towards Milton of Campsie.

 Surface + Hills: Stone and gravel path. Gentle downhill from Strathblane to Kirkintilloch.

Roads + Road crossings: Two minor roads to cross. Short section on road through Kirkintilloch.

Links or other nearby trails: The Forth & Clyde Canal runs through Kirkintilloch. There is another long railway path between Airdrie and Bathgate.

 Map + Leaflet: OS Landranger Map 64.

 Refreshments: Strathblane, Lennoxtown, Milton of Campsie and Kirkintilloch.

Nearest Railway: Milngavie (south of Strathblane) or Auchinloch (south of Kirkintilloch).

240. SUTTON PARK, north of Birmingham

There are plans to improve all of the Birmingham Canal Network, including the tow-paths running alongside the waterways. Until this happens, the official policy is that cycling is only allowed on the Birmingham Main Line Canal which links the centres of Birmingham and Wolverhampton. So... for traffic–free cycling near to Birmingham try the forest trails at **Cannock Chase**, the **Kingswinford Railway Walk** or the trails through Sutton Park.

 Route and distance: There are several miles of tracks and bridle-ways through Sutton Park. Use the map available from the Visitor Centre to plan your routes around the park.

Category: Country park trails.

Start + Parking: Sutton Park Visitor Centre, off the A5127 on the west side of Sutton Coldfield.

 Surface + Hills: Stone and gravel paths. Gentle hills.

Roads + Road crossings: None, once you have left the estate roads.

Links or other nearby trails: The **Birmingham & Black Country Canal Cycleway** links the city centres of Birmingham and Wolverhampton. The **Kingswinford Railway Walk** runs from Pensnett (west of Dudley) to Aldersley Stadium, north of Wolverhampton. Several waymarked trails in **Cannock Chase**.

Map + Leaflet: OS Landranger Map . Leaflet available from the Visitor Centre, Sutton Park, Sutton Coldfield, West Midlands. B74 2YT. Tel: 0121 355 6370. A comprehensive cyclists' map of Birmingham is produced by CycleCity Guides which shows all the city's recreational routes and best commuter routes. Available by sending £4.95 payable to CycleCity Guides, Wallbridge Mill, The Retreat, Frome BA11 5JU. Tel: 01373 453533.

 Refreshments:
At the Visitor Centre.

Nearest Railway: Sutton Coldfield.

241. SWANSEA CANAL,
northeast of Swansea, South Wales
In their heyday the Neath and Swansea Canals brought thousands of tons of coal down from the pits in the Swansea Valley and the Vale of Neath. Both were superceded by the railways and now plans have been drawn up to restore both waterways.

 The route: Clydach (north of Swansea) – Pontardawe – Ynysmeudwy.

Distance: 6 miles one way, 12 miles return.

Category: Canal towpath.

Start + Parking: Clydach, on the B4603 to the north of M4 Jct 45. The canal starts at the junction of the River Tawe with the Lower Clydach River. Or in Ynysmeudwy, at the roundabout by the junction of the A4067 with the B4603.

 Surface + Hills: Mixed quality – some good gravel stretches, some rougher, narrower sections. No hills.

Roads + Road crossings: Short road sec-

---

tion in Pontardawe.

Links or other nearby trails: There are two good cyclepaths in **Swansea**. The **Neath Canal** runs along the next valley to the east. There are several waymarked trails starting at the **Afan Argoed Country Park** (northeast of Port Talbot).

 Map + Leaflet: OS Landranger Maps 160 + 170.

 Refreshments: In Clydach and Pontardawe.

Nearest Railway: Swansea or Neath.

242. SWANSEA BIKEPATH
(along the seafront)
The wide curving sweep of Swansea Bay is the perfect setting for a bike path and by good fortune (and visionary planning) such a path exists running from Mumbles round to the Maritime Quarter in the centre of the city.

 The route: The Maritime Quarter (Swansea City Centre) – University – Blackpill – Oystermouth – Mumbles.

Distance: 5 miles one way, 10 miles both.

Category: Railway path/ seafront promenade.

Start + Parking: The Maritime Quarter in the centre of Swansea. Parking also available opposite the University and in Mumbles.

 Surface + Hills: Tarmac path. No hills.

Roads + Road crossings: None.

Links or other nearby trails: There is a link up the Clyne valley (**Swansea – Clyne**

Valley). A section of the **Swansea Canal** towpath can be ridden.

 Map + Leaflet: OS Landranger Map 159. Leaflet available from Swansea Tourist Information Centre. Tel: 01792 468321.

 Refreshments: In the Maritime Quarter or in Mumbles.

Nearest Railway: Swansea.

243. SWANSEA AND THE CLYNE VALLEY

A spur leads off the main seafront cyclepath alongside the Clyne River providing a delightful wooded trail that runs northwest to Gowerton. This forms part of a Sustrans route that will run from Kidwelly (west of Llanelli) through Swansea and Pontypridd to Newport.

 The route: Blackpill – Clyne Valley Country Park – Dunvant – Gowerton.

Distance: 5 miles one way, 10 miles both.

Category: Railway path.

Start + Parking: Best to use the seafront bike path to access the start of the Clyne Valley Spur at Blackpill. Parking in Mumbles or opposite the University on the main road around Swansea Bay (A4067).

 Surface + Hills: Gravel path. Steady 300 ft climb from the coast to the highpoint between Dunvant and Gowerton.

Roads + Road crossings: Use the pelican crossing to cross the main road at Blackpill.

Links or other nearby trails: The **Swansea Bikepath** runs along the seafront from the Maritime Quarter to Mumbles.

 Map + Leaflet: OS Landranger Map 159. A leaflet is available from Swansea Tourist Information Centre.

 Refreshments: In Dunvant and Gowerton.

Nearest Railway: Swansea or Gowerton.

SWINDON RAILWAY PATH – see 219. **River Ray Parkway**

244. TAFF TRAIL (part of Sustrans Welsh National Route)

A long trail – built by the local Groundwork Trust – that uses a mixture of riverside path, forestry tracks, railway paths and minor lanes to link the centre of Cardiff with the centre of Brecon, passing through Pontypridd and Merthyr Tydfil.

 The Route: Cardiff – Castell Coch – Pontypridd – Abercynon – Aberfan – Merthyr Tydfil – Pontsticill – Talybont on Usk – Llanfrynach – Brecon.

Distance: 53 miles one way from Cardiff to Brecon.

Category: Sustrans National Cycle Network Route with a mixture of railway paths, minor lanes and woodland trails.

Traffic–free sections:
1. Cardiff College of Music and Drama on North Road (just north of Cardiff Castle on the A470 towards Merthyr Tydfil) to Tongwynlais (5 miles).

2. Castell Coch to Glyntaff Cemetery, south-east of Pontypridd (6 miles).

3. Navigation Inn, Abercynon (near junction of A470 and B4275) to the Rhydycar Leisure Centre, Merthyr Tydfil (9 miles).

4. Cefn Coed (north of Merthyr Tydfil, just east of the junction of the A465 and A470) to Pontsticill (4 miles).

From Pontsticill to Brecon (22 miles) the route is much tougher and more beautiful, using a mixture of minor lanes and forestry tracks.

Start + Parking: At the Cardiff College of Music and Drama; Castell Coch; Rhydycar Leisure Centre (Merthyr Tydfil); Pontsticill Reservoir; Llanfrynach; Brecon.

 Surface + Hills: Tarmac, fine gravel path, forestry track. Gentle 1000 ft climb over 30 miles from Cardiff to Pontsticill Reservoir, north of Merthyr Tydfil. Beyond this there are several road climbs. There is one unexpectedly very steep section near to Castell Coch.

Roads + Road crossings: Several road crossings and road sections. The busy sections to avoid are:

1. The A4054 between Glyntaff Cemetery and Abercynon.

2. The roads through Merthyr Tydfil. These sections will be improved in the future.

Links or other nearby trails: The Taff Trail is part of Sustrans Welsh National Route (National Cycle Network) from Cardiff to Holyhead on Anglesey. Beyond Brecon the route continues to Builth Wells, Llanidloes, Machynlleth, Dolgellau, Criccieth and Caernarfon. The two canals north of Newport have excellent towpaths. Throughout South Wales there are vast holdings of Forestry Commission land with lots of waymarked trails.

Cycle Hire:
Taff Trail Cycle Hire, Forest Farm Country Park, Whitchurch, Cardiff. 01222 751235.

Bikes and Hikes, Y Llyfen, 10 The Street, Brecon LD3 7LL. Tel: 01874 610071.

 Map + Leaflet: OS Landranger Maps 160, 161, 170, 171. Set of 6 free leaflets available from: The Taff Trail Project, Groundwork Merthyr & Cynon, Fedw Hir, Llwydcoed, Aberdare, CF44 0DX. Tel: 01685 883880.

 Refreshments: Lots of choice along the way.

Nearest Railway: Lots of stations between Cardiff and Merthyr Tydfil. None beyond. A good trip would be to take the train from Cardiff to Merthyr Tydfil then cycle gently downhill back to Cardiff.

245. TAME VALLEY TRAIL AND THE DELPH DONKEY, NW of Manchester

Follow the River Tame, a tributary of the River Mersey down its steep-sided valley along the course of an old railway line that used to serve the mills. There is plenty of architectural interest against a background of moorland scenery.

 The route: Brownhill Visitor Centre, Uppermill (east of Oldham) – Greenfield – The Roaches – Mossley.

Distance: 3 miles one way, 6 miles both.

Category: Railway path.

Start + Parking: Brownhill Visitor Centre, Uppermill, on the A670, 5 miles east of east of Oldham (Manchester).

 Surface + Hills: Crushed sandstone and fine gravel. Short steep sections to get on to the path from Brownhill.

Roads + Road crossings: Take care crossing the A670 from Brownhills Visitor Centre and the A669 at Greenfield near The Roaches.

Links or other nearby trails: The route is likely to be extended down the Tame Valley via Stalybridge to the Ashton Canal.

 Map + Leaflet: OS Landranger Map 109. Leaflet available from Tame Valley Countryside Warden Service. Tel: 0161 3423306.

 Refreshments: Lots of pubs and cafes in Uppermill and Delph. Pubs in Greenfield and Mossley.

Nearest Railway: Greenfield and Mossley, each 0.5 mile from the Tame Valley Trail.

246. TARKA TRAIL, Barnstaple, Devon
A magnificent railway path from the heart of Devon to the north coast along the estuaries of the Rivers Taw and Torridge, passing through the historic town of Barnstaple. The trail forms part of Sustrans West Country Way which runs from Padstow to Bristol.

NB The DevonBus Service 361 carries bikes and enables you to cycle one way and catch a bus back to your starting point. Tel: 01392 382800, 01271 382800 or 01752 382800.

 The route: Meeth – Petrockstowe (12 miles northeast of Okehampton) – Great Torrington – Instow – Bideford – Barnstaple – Braunton.

Distance: Anything up to 33 miles one way, 66 miles round trip.

Category: Railway path.

Start + Parking: Several possible starting points: Meeth, Petrockstowe, East Yarde,

Torrington, East-the-Water, Instow, Barnstaple, Braunton.

 Surface + Hills: Stone/gravel path. Steady 200 ft climb from Torrington to Petrockstowe.

Roads + Road crossings: There is a short section on roads through Barnstaple to link the route along the south side of the Taw estuary (from Instow) to the route along the north side of the estuary to Braunton.

Other nearby trails: The Tarka Trail forms part of two sections of Sustrans National Cycle Network – the West Country Way (Padstow to Bristol, 250 miles) and the Devon Coast to Coast Route (Plymouth to Ilfracombe, 90 miles). There is a woodland trail at Eggesford (12 miles northeast of Crediton on the A377). There is also a good route from Torrington Station towards Watergate, the old Rolle canal following the river Torridge. At Watergate turn right through Rolle tunnel and left to the old Creamery. Cross the main road at Taddiport and rejoin Rolle Road on to Town Mills (check out the view from Castle Hill).

Cycle Hire:
Otter Cycle Hire, Braunton. tel: 01271 813339; Bideford Cycle Hire 01237 424123; Tarka Trail Cycle Hire at Barnstaple railway station. 01271 324202.

 Map + Leaflet: OS Landranger Maps 180 + 191. Pack of laminated route cards can be purchased from Tarka Country Tourism Association. Tel: 01837 345008.

 Refreshments: Puffing Billy pub at Torrington, lots of choice in Bideford and Barnstaple.

Nearest Railway: Barnstaple.

247. TATTON PARK,
northwest of Knutsford, Cheshire

There is a charge to enter this country estate by car so there is very little traffic on the estate roads within the park. As a result it is a fine place to cycle through the attractive parkland which has been a refuge for deer for hundreds of years.

 Route and distance: There are 8 miles of estate roads within Tatton Park. It is suggested that you explore wherever takes your fancy, staying on the surfaced roads.

Category: Estate roads.

Start + Parking: Follow signs off the A556 which runs between Junction 7/8 of the M56 and Junction 19 of the M6 between Altrincham and Knutsford. There is a charge to enter the park.

 Surface + Hills: Tarmac. Gently undulating.

Roads + Road crossings: There is traffic on the estate roads but it is travelling slowly and signs tell motorists to beware of cyclists. More traffic during summer weekends, so plan accordingly.

Links or other nearby trails: The Middlewood Way (from Marple to Macclesfield) lies 8 miles to the east.

Cycle Hire: In Tatton Park, near the restaurant. Tel: 01625 572681.

 Map + Leaflet: OS Landranger Map 109 and 118. The park also produces a map.

 Refreshments: Restaurants and refreshments near the mansion.

Nearest Railway: Knutsford.

248. TEST WAY,
Stockbridge, Hampshire

Stockbridge is a large attractive village on the River Test, one of the best fishing rivers in the country. The railway path follows the river southwards for over 5 miles, although you do not see the river as much as you might expect.

 The route: Stockbridge – valley of the River Test – Horsebridge – A3057 at Stonymarsh car park.

Distance: 5.5 miles one way, 11 miles both.

Category: Railway path.

Start + Parking: Trafalgar Way, off the roundabout at the eastern end of Stockbridge at the junction of the A30 and A3057. (The White Hart pub is situated on the roundabout).

 Surface + Hills: Stone/gravel path, no hills.

Roads + Road crossings: One quiet lane to cross at Horsebridge. The trail ends at Stonymarsh car park. Do not be tempted to go beyond onto the dangerous, busy A3057.

Links or other nearby trails: The long distance bridleway, the **South Downs Way**, starts in Winchester, 10 miles southeast of Stockbridge.

 Map + Leaflet: OS Landranger Map 185.

 Refreshments: Lots of choice in Stockbridge. Try the John of Gaunt pub by the River Test at Stockbridge.

Nearest Railway: Mottisfont.

249. THAMES TOWPATH between Putney Bridge and Weybridge

A magnificent ride alongside Britain's most famous river, passing many London sights along the way.

 The route: Putney Bridge – Kew – Richmond – Kingston – Hampton Court – Walton on Thames – Weybridge

Distance: Anything up to 24 miles one way, 48 miles return.

Category: Riverside path.

Start + Parking: Kew Gardens, Kingston, Ham Lands (opposite Eel Pie Island), Richmond. Walton Bridge, Walton-on-Thames.

 Surface + Hills: Good quality stone-based and gravel path.

Roads + Road crossings: Two main roads to cross, one at Kingston Bridge and one at Hampton Court Bridge. Both have pedestrian crossings at the northern end of the bridges. It is worth using these even though it means walking away from the river before walking back the other side.

Links or other nearby trails: Can be linked via the **Wey Navigation** to the **Basingstoke Canal** forming a 50 mile route from Putney Bridge almost to Basingstoke in deepest Hampshire! There is a trail in **Richmond Park.**

 Map + Leaflet: OS Landranger Map 176. Better to use a coloured A–Z map of London.

 Refreshments: All along the way.

Nearest Railway: Several railway stations along the route,

250. THETFORD FOREST, Thetford, northwest of Cambridge

Two waymarked trails in this large forestry holding. There are plenty of options for exploring further with the aid of a map.

 The routes, distance, start and parking:

1. Brandon Park Loop, 6.5 miles. Start at Mayday Farm car park (off B1106)

2. High Lodge Loop. 6.5 miles. Start at High Lodge Forest Centre, on the Forest Drive, off the B1107 east of Brandon

Category: Forest trails.

 Surface + Hills: Stone and gravel forestry tracks. Gentle hills.

Roads + Road crossings: If you link the two routes there is a crossing of the busy (and fast) B1106. Take great care with young children.

Links or other nearby trails: The **Peddars Way** is a long distance trail that runs north from Thetford to the Norfolk Coast.

Cycle Hire: At High Lodge Forest Centre. Tel: 01842 815434.

 Map + Leaflet: OS Landranger Maps 143 + 144. Much better is the Forest Enterprise map, available from the Forest Centre or from Forest District, Santon Downham, Brandon, Suffolk. IP27 0TJ. Tel: 01842 810271.

 Refreshments: At the Forest Centre.

Nearest Railway: Brandon.

251. THREE FOREST CYCLE TRAIL,
northeast of Ipswich, Suffolk

This ride links three forests near to the Suffolk Coast using a mixture of roads and forest trails. If you wish to avoid roads altogether then stick to the tracks in Tunstall and Rendlesham Forests.

 The route: Forest Enterprise Offices, Rendlesham Forest – Butley – Chillesford – Tunstall Forest – Snape – Aldeburgh – Aldringham – Eastbridge – Dunwich.

Distance: 25 miles one way. (The forestry sections are much shorter).

Category: Forest trails and roads. There are busier roads on the section north of Snape.

Start + Parking: Tangham House (Forest Enterprise car park), Rendlesham Forest, east of Ipswich. Leave the A12 at Woodbridge, northeast of Ipswich. Follow the A1152 then the B1084 towards Butley. After 4 miles on the B1084, take the first road to the right.

 Surface + Hills: Tarmac and forest roads. No hills.

Roads + Road crossings: In its entirety the Three Forests Cycle Trail is more road than offroad. There are trails to follow in Rendlesham and Tunstall Forests and it is recommended going as far as the Snape Maltings which are well worth visiting.

Links or other nearby trails: Alton Water Reservoir is just south of Ipswich.

 Map + Leaflet: OS Landranger Maps 156 + 169. A Forest Enterprise leaflet is available from East Anglia Forest District, Santon Downham, Brandon, Suffolk. IP27 0TJ. Tel: 01842 810271.

 Refreshments: In Butley, Sudbourne, Snape, Aldeburgh, Eastbridge and Dunwich.

Nearest Railway: Market Wickham Station.

TISSINGTON TRAIL – see 126 – 127. High Peak and Tissington

TOBERMORY – see 282– 285. West of Scotland Forestry

TRANS PENNINE TRAIL (from west to east)
see: Cheshire Lines Path; Liverpool Loop Line; Sankey Valley Park & St Helen's Canal; Warrington to Altrincham; River Mersey through South Manchester; Longdendale Trail; Dove Valley Trail

The 200-mile Trans Pennine Trail is due to open this year. It links up many of the above existing trails so can be part ridden now. Become a Friend of the TPT and you get a newsletter and events information. It costs £6 pa for individuals and £10 pa for families. Details from Trevor Blackburn, 164 High Street, Hook, Goole DN14 5PL.

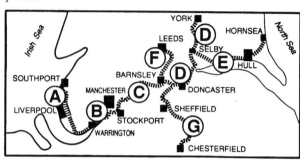

252 – 258. TWEED VALLEY FORESTRY
(Glentress, Cardrona, Elibank and Traquair)
There are many miles of forest trails in this lovely part of Scotland, looking down on the magnificent River Tweed as it winds its majestic course down to the sea at Berwick.

DISTANCE	GRADE	MARKERS	START & CAR PARK
A. GLENTRESS FOREST			
252. Anderson			
3 miles	Moderate	Red	Falla Brae car park, off the A72, east of Peebles
253. Dunslair			
11 miles	Demanding	Blue	
B. CARDRONA FOREST			
254. Highlandshiel's			
4.5 miles	Easy	Red	Kirkburn car park, off the B7602, SE of Peebles
255. Wallace's Hill			
7.5 miles	Moderate	Green	
C. ELIBANK AND TRAQUAIR			
256. Touring Route			
12 miles	Easy	Yellow	Plora Entrance car park, off the minor road parallel with A72 east of Innerleithen
257. Cheesewell			
8.5 miles	Moderate	Green	
258. Minch Moor			
14.5 miles	Demanding	Blue	

 Surface + Hills: Forestry tracks, lots of hills. **Refreshments**: In Peebles

Railway: No nearby railway.

259. UNION CANAL,
west of Edinburgh

One of two canals that enters Edinburgh from the west (the other is the Water of Leith). The route is not continuous so be prepared to use a street map to link the missing sections.

 The route: South of Falkirk (Glen Village) – Linlithgow – Broxbourn – Ratho – Edinburgh (with some missing sections!)

Distance: 30 miles one way, 60 miles round trip. (You will need to use road sections if you intend to cover the whole length of the canal).

Category: Canal towpath.

Start + Parking: The towpath starts in Edinburgh at the junction of Gilmore Park and Dundee Street (southwest of the Castle). It stops near to Kingsknowe Station, then starts again west of Wester Hailes near the junction of Calder Road with the ring road.

 Surface + Hills: Stone and gravel path, some rougher, rutted sections. No hills.

Roads + Road crossings: You will need to use some road sections to cover the missing links in the canal. It is best to take a street map with you for this purpose.

Links or other nearby trails: The **Water of Leith** also has a towpath. There is a cyclepath between **Newbridge and the Forth Bridge**.

 Map + Leaflet: OS Landranger Maps 65 + 66. An excellent cyclists' map of Edinburgh can be purchased from SPOKES, The Lothian Cycle Campaign, St Martin's Church, 232 Dalry Road, Edinburgh. EH1 2JG. Tel: 0131 313 2114.

 Refreshments: All along the way.

Nearest Railway: Edinburgh, Slateford, Kingsknowe, Linlithgow, Polmont, Falkirk.

260. UPPER DERWENT VALLEY RESERVOIRS, between Manchester and Sheffield

A magnificent ride amid the beauty of woodland, lakes and moorland alongside the reservoirs in the Upper Derwent Valley.

 The route: Various routes possible from the Ladybower Reservoir (Fairholmes) Visitor Centre – circuits of one, two or three of the reservoirs, or a there-and back ride along the west side of Derwent and Howden Reservoirs.

Distance: Anything from 5 miles (circuit of the northern part of Ladybower) to 16 miles (circuit of all three reservoirs).

Category: Round reservoir route.

Start + Parking: Turn off the A57 Sheffield to Glossop road on the west side of the viaduct over Ladybower Reservoir. The Visitor Centre lies 2.5 miles up this road.

 Surface + Hills: Mixture of tarmac, fine stone tracks and slightly rougher tracks on the east side of Howden Reservoir. Several small climbs.

Roads + Road crossings: The road from the A57 to the Visitor Centre carries a reasonable amount of traffic at the height of the season, but the cars are probably carrying other cyclists to get to the start!

Links or other nearby trails: The **Longdendale Trail** is just north of Glossop.

Cycle Hire: At the Visitor Centre. Tel: 01433 651261.

 Map + Leaflet: OS Landranger Map 110 or Outdoor Leisure Map no. 1.

 Refreshments: Hot drinks, cakes and sweets available at the Visitor Centre.

Nearest Railway: Hope Station is south of Ladybower Reservoir.

261. VALLEY WALK, Sudbury, northwest of Colchester

One of few dismantled railways in Suffolk that has been converted to recreational use, this one follows the delightful River Stour which forms the boundary between Suffolk and Essex for much of its length.

 The route: Leisure Pool, Sudbury northwest for 3 miles parallel to the River Stour to Rodbridge (B1064 west of Rodbridge Corner).

Distance: 3 miles one way, 6 miles return.

Category: Railway path.

Start + Parking: The trail starts opposite the main entrance to the Leisure Pool in Sudbury, 15 miles NW of Colchester. Look out for a 'Valley Walk' sign at the start of the trail. There is a car park at the Leisure Pool.

 Surface + Hills: Stone and gravel path. No hills.

Roads + Road crossings: None, unless you choose to explore the lanes beyond the end of the path to get to the village pubs.

Links or other nearby trails: The circuit of Alton Water is just south of Ipswich.

 Map + Leaflet: OS Landranger Map 155.

 Refreshments: Lots of choice in Sudbury. There are pubs in the villages a few miles along quiet lanes from the end of the railway path.

Nearest Railway: Sudbury (the route starts from the station).

262. WARRINGTON TO ALTRINCHAM (between Manchester and Liverpool)

A ride along the former London and North Western Railway and part of the Manchester Ship Canal from Warrington to Altrincham. This forms part of the Trans Pennine Trail which, when complete, will run from the West Coast at Southport, through Liverpool and Manchester to the East Coast at Hull.

The route: Latchford Lock on the Manchester Ship Canal (southeast Warrington) – Lymm – the River Bollin at Altrincham.

Distance: 5 miles one way, 10 miles both.

Category: Railway path and canal towpath.

Start + Parking: The Manchester Ship Canal at London Road, Stockton Heath, on the south side of Warrington (A49 north of M56 Jct 10). Heatley, on the A6144, north-east of Lymm (east of M6 Jct 21).

Surface + Hills: Gravel path. No hills.

Roads + Road crossings: Minor road crossings in Lymm.

Links or other nearby trails: This is part of the Trans Pennine Trail. To the west is **Sankey Valley Park & St Helens Canal**, to the east there is a section still to be built to link to Sale Water Park **(Mersey River through South Manchester)**

Map + Leaflet: OS Landranger Map 109. Leaflets covering all the Trans Pennine Trail are available from the Trans Pennine Trail Officer, c/o Planning Services, Barnsley MBC, Central Offices, Kendray Street, Barnsley, S70 2TN. Tel: 01226 772574.

Refreshments: Several pubs just off the route.

Nearest Railway: Warrington or Altrincham.

263. WASKERLEY WAY, south of Consett, County Durham
A dramatic route which climbs from industrial Consett into the heart of the Durham Dales with fine views across the wild moors and

remote reservoirs.

The route: Hownsgill Viaduct (south of Consett) – Rowley – Waskerley – B6278 at Weatherhill Summit (north of Stanhope).

Distance: 9.5 miles one way, 19 miles both.

Category: Railway path.

Start + Parking: Hownsgill Viaduct car park, signposted off the A692 between Consett and Castleside. Also at Rowley Station, Waskerly picnic site and Meeting Slacks.

Surface + Hills: Stony/grassy path. Mountain bikes recommended. Steady 900 ft climb all the way from Consett to Weatherhill summit (on the B6278). Steep descent to Stanhope, if you choose to go down here for refreshments.

Roads + Road crossings: Sections of the relatively busy B6278 into Stanhope.

Links or other nearby trails: The trail joins three other cycle routes at Hownes Gill Viaduct – the **Consett to Sunderland Railway Path**, the **Derwent Walk** and the **Lanchester Valley Walk**.

Cycle Hire:
Weardale Mountain Bikes, tel: 01388 528129.

Map + Leaflet: OS Landranger Maps 87 + 88 (+ 92 if you are going into Stanhope). A fine set of laminated route cards covering 7 railway paths in County Durham can be purchased from The Countryside Group, Environment & Technical Services Dept., Durham County Council, County Hall, Durham. DH1 5UQ. Tel: 0191 383 4144.

Refreshments: Pubs and cafes in Consett and Stanhope.

Nearest Railway: Prudhoe (to the north), Chester-le-Street or Durham (to the east), all 10-12 miles from the start, although much of this is on railway paths.

264. WATER OF LEITH,
East of Edinburgh
Although the waterway can be followed north and east through Edinburgh it becomes very bitty with frequent road sections. The best part runs from Kingsknowe to Balerno, passing the many old mills which used the water from the river as a source of power.

 The route: Union Canal Bridge (Kingsknowe) – Colinton – Currie – Balerno.

Distance: 6 miles one way, 12 miles both.

Category: Canal towpath.

Start + Parking: The Union Canal Bridge, on the Lanark Road (A70) just to the east of Kingsknowe Railway Station on the west side of Edinburgh. Or in Balerno (just off the A70 on the north side of the village).

 Surface + Hills: Stone and gravel path. Steady climb from Kingsknowe to Balerno.

Roads + Road crossings: Several short sections of quiet road are used to link together the canal towpath.

Links or other nearby trails: The Union Canal also runs into the east side of Edinburgh. There is a cyclepath betwen Newbridge and the Forth Road Bridge.

 Map + Leaflet: OS Landranger Map 66. An excellent cyclists' map of Edinburgh can be purchased

from SPOKES, The Lothian Cycle Campaign, St Martin's Church, 232 Dalry Road, Edinburgh. EH1 2JG. Tel: 0131 313 2114.

 Refreshments: Lots of choice all along the route.

Nearest Railway: Edinburgh, Currie.

265. WAYFARERS WALK (1),
south of Newbury, Berkshire
Although this is essentially a long distance walk, there are some sections which have bridleway or byway status where you are allowed to cycle. There are fantastic views from the ridge. The ride should only be undertaken on mountain bikes, during the summer months, with the appropriate Ordnance Survey map.

 The route: White Hill (B3051 south of Kingsclere) – Watership Down – A34 – Ashmansworth – Walbury Hill – Inkpen Hill – Ham Hill – Botley Down.

Distance: 18 miles one way, 36 miles both.

Category: Long distance trail.

Start + Parking: White Hill car park on the B3051, 2 miles south of Kingsclere.

 Surface + Hills: Stone-based, muddy in winter and after prolonged rain. Several hills.

Roads + Road crossings: Several crossings of minor roads. Short sections of lanes are used. There is a permissive bridleway route that crosses the A34 safely. Follow the signs.

Links or other nearby trails: The Kennet & Avon Canal runs west from Hungerford (Froxfield) to Bath.

 Map + Leaflet: OS Landranger Maps 174 + 185. Leaflet available from Countryside Dept.,

Hampshire County Council, Mottisfont Court, High Street, Winchester. SO23 8ZF. Tel: 01962 846045.

Refreshments: Pubs in Kingsclere and Ashmansworth.

Nearest Railway: Great Bedwyn is 4 miles north of the western end of the trail.

266. WAYFARERS WALK (2), south of Basingstoke, Hampshire

A second section of the long distance trail through the beautiful rolling chalk downland of Hampshire, running north from the attractive town of New Alresford to Dummer, south of Basingstoke. The ride should only be undertaken on mountain bikes, during the summer months, with the appropriate OS map.

The route: New Alresford – Brown Candover – Dummer (southwest of Basingstoke).

Distance: 13 miles one way, 26 miles both.

Category: Long distance trail

Start + Parking: The main car park near the railway station in New Alresford, 10 miles east of Winchester.

Surface + Hills: Bridleways and byways with some rough sections. Muddy in winter and after prolonged rain. Undulating terrain.

Roads + Road crossings: Several short stretches on roads including a busier section at the start in New Alresford.

Links or other nearby trails: The **South Downs Way** is another long distance bridleway. The **Meon Valley Trail** is a railway path starting in West Meon, southeast of New Alresford.

Map + Leaflet: OS Landranger Map 185. Leaflet available from Countryside Dept., Hampshire County Council.

Refreshments: Lots of choice in New Alresford. Pub in Dummer.

Nearest Railway: Micheldever Station.

267. WEAVERS WAY, North Walsham, Norfolk

Running along the course of a dismantled railway through attractive woodland and verges full of wildflowers in spring and summer, the Weavers Way can easily be linked to the Marriotts Way to form one of the longest railway path rides in the country.

The route: North Walsham west to Aylsham.

Distance: 6 miles one way, 12 miles both.

Category: Railway path.

Start + Parking: Small car park on Station Road, half a mile to the west of the railway station, on the west side of North Walsham.

Surface + Hills: Stone and gravel path. Short rough section if you go beyond the end of the railway path into Aylsham. No hills.

Roads + Road crossings: Several minor roads to cross. One major road (the A140) must be crossed if you go into Aylsham.

Links or other nearby trails: The **Marriotts Way** starts at Aylsham and heads west to Reepham before swinging southeast to Norwich.

Map + Leaflet: OS Landranger Map 133. Leaflet available from the Planning and Transportation Department, Norfolk County Council, County Hall, Martineau Lane, Norwich. NR1 2DH.

Refreshments: Lots of choice in North Walsham and Aylsham.

Nearest Railway: North Walsham.

268 – 285 WEST OF SCOTLAND FORESTRY (18 routes)

A whole series of forestry routes waymarked by the Forestry Commission in their holdings lying to the west of a line from Glasgow to Fort William. Many have spectacular views of the lochs, coastline and islands in this magnificent part of Scotland. See also **Argyll Forest Park** *for routes in the region between the A82 and Loch Fyne, northwest of Glasgow.*

DISTANCE	GRADE	MARKERS	START & CAR PARK
268. Ballochgair			
14 miles	Hard	Blue	Ballochgair car park on the B842 Carradale Road north of Campbeltown
269. Ardnoe			
13 miles	Hard	Blue	Druim-an-Duin car park off the B8025 Tayvallich road, 20 miles south of Oban, off the A816
270. Faery Isles			
6 miles	Easy	Red	Druim–an–Duin car park off the B8025 Tayvallich road, 20 miles south of Oban, off the A816
271. Lochan Buic			
11 miles	Hard	Green	Dunardry car park, near Cairnbaan on the B841, 20 miles south of Oban, off the A816
272. Kilmory to Carrick			
6 miles	Easy	Blue	Kilmory Castle car park, near Lochgilphead, 25 miles south of Oban, south of A816 / A83 junction
273. Loch Glashan (Ardcastle)			
9 miles	Easy	Purple & Red	Ardcastle car park, on the A83 north of Lochgilphead
274. Ormaig			
9 miles	Medium	Purple	Carnasserie Castle car park, on the A816, 15 miles south of Oban
275. Two Lochs			
9 miles	Easy	Green	Barnaline car park, on the minor road on the west side of Loch Awe, at the road junction east of Loch Avich (southeast of Oban)
276. Glen Orchy			
8 miles	Hard	Red	Car park at Bridge of Orchy, on the A82 between Crianlarich and Fort William

DISTANCE	GRADE	MARKERS	START & CAR PARK

277. Fearnoch & Glen Lonan

5 miles	Easy	Red & Green	Quarry car park in forest east of Fearnoch village on the A85 between Connel and Taynuilt (northeast of Oban)

278. Mill Farm & Barcaldine

8 miles	Easy	Red & Purple	Forest car park 1 mile south of Barcaldine, on the A828 northeast of Oban

279. Glen Dubh

5 miles	Easy	Blue	Sutherland's Grove car park, 0.5 mile north east of Barcaldine on the A828 northeast of Oban
8 miles	Medium	Green	

280. Glenachulish & St Johns

6 miles	Easy	Blue & Red	Car park in Glenachulish, 1/4 mile west of the Ballachulish Bridge on the A82 Oban road. (East of the A82 / A828 junction)

281. Leanachan Forest

Lots!	All grades.		Aonach Mor ski facility, 6 miles north of Fort William

282. Head of Loch Aline & Savary

9 miles	Medium	Red	Lochaline, at the end of the A884, 40 miles southwest of Fort William

283. Head of Loch Aline & Arienas

3.5 miles	Easy	Blue	Loch Arienas, off the A884, 4 miles north of Locahaline (40 miles southwest of Fort William)

284. Lettermore & Loch Frisa

5 miles	Easy	Blue	Aros Forest Office, on the A848, 10
16 miles	Easy	Red	miles southeast of Tobermory, Isle of Mull

285. Ardmore & Glengorm

4 miles	Easy	Red	Forest car park 2 miles along the minor road from Tobermory towards Glengorm

Map + Leaflet: OS Landranger maps 41, 47, 48, 49, 50, 55, 56, 62 + 68. Much better is the leaflet produced by the Forestry Commission – *Cycling in the Forest – West of Scotland,* available from Lochaber Forest District, Torlundy, Fort William, Inverness–shire, PH33 6SW. Tel: 01397 702184.

286. WEST WALK FOREST,
northwest of Portsmouth.
A short waymarked forest trail in what used to be the huge Forest of Bere, used for hunting by Saxon Kings, then the Normans. Charles I was the last monarch to hunt here and even by then (1628) the forest was greatly reduced, much of the wood being used to make ships in nearby Portsmouth.

 The route, distance and category: 3 mile long waymarked forest trail.

Start + Parking: Forest car park on the minor road towards Soberton Heath, off the A32 (the Fareham – Alton road), 3 miles north of Wickham.

 Surface + Hills: Forest tracks, gentle climbs.

Roads + Road crossings: One crossing of a minor road.

Links or other nearby trails: The Meon Valley Trail starts in Wickham. There are many miles of trails in the New Forest.

 Map + Leaflet: OS Landranger Map 196. Leaflet available from Forest Enterprise, Buck Horn Oak, Farnham, Surrey. GU10 4LS. Tel: 01420 23666.

 Refreshments: Lots of choice in Wickham.

Nearest Railway: Fareham or Botley.

287. WEY NAVIGATION, Surrey.
The Wey Navigation and the Basingstoke Canal both start to the southwest of London, join at West Byfleet and continue on to Weybridge to join the Thames Towpath. You go right though urban areas but wouldn't know it, the towpath being a slice of country life.

 The route: Godalming – Guildford – Byfleet – Weybridge.

Distance: 16 miles one way, 32 miles both.

Category: Canal towpath.

Start + Parking: Just south of Guildford, off the A281 towards Shalford. Also on the B367 between Ripley and West Byfleet where the road crosses the canal.

 Surface + Hills: Mixture. Some good, stone and gravel sections, others rougher and narrower.

Links or other nearby trails: The Wey Navigation joins the Thames Towpath at Weybridge and can be followed to Putney Bridge in London. It joins the Basingstoke Canal at West Byfleet.

 Map + Leaflet: OS Landranger Maps 176, 186 + 187.

 Refreshments: Lots of choice in Guildford and Weybridge. Pub at Cartbridge (near Old Woking) and several more just off the route.

Nearest Railway: Godalming, Guildford, Brooklands.

288. WHINLATTER FOREST PARK,
west of Keswick, Cumbria
Two waymarked routes on steep woodland trails through this spectacularly set Forestry Commission holding west of Keswick.

 Route: The short loop is way-marked with orange bike signs, the longer route with purple bike signs.

Distance: 5 miles and 7 miles.

Category: Forest trail.

Start + Parking: The Visitor Centre on the B5292 between Keswick and Cockermouth.

 Surface + Hills: Stone and gravel forest track. Lots of steep hills!

Roads + Road crossings: The B5292 must be crossed on both loops.

Links or other nearby trails: Keswick Railway Path, Whitehaven Railway Path.

 Map + Leaflet: OS Landranger Map 89. Leaflet (£1.25) can be purchased from Whinlatter Forest Park, Braithwaite, Keswick. CA12 5TW. Tel: 017687 78469.

 Refreshments: At the Visitor Centre.

Nearest Railway: Workington.

289. WHITEGATE WAY,
east of Chester
From sand pit to salt mine, this railway path route crosses the sedimentary geology of the Cheshire Plain, lying between the Clwyd Hills to the west and the Peak District to the east. The trail can be explored to the east and west from the car park/picnic site at Marton Green.

 The route: Cuddington (Oakmere Hall, on the A556, 4 miles west of Northwich) to the minor road from Winsford N to Whitegate.

Distance: 6 miles one way, 12 miles both.

Category: Railway path.

Start + Parking: Marton Green, on the minor road between Cuddington (A556) and Winsford (A54), 10 miles west of M6 junction 18.

 Surface + Hills: Stone and gravel path. Gentle climb from east to west.

Roads + Road crossings: No major road crossings.

Links or other nearby trails: Delamere Forest Trails.

 Map + Leaflet: OS Landranger Map 117 + 118. Leaflet available from The Rangers' Office, Linmere Picnic Site, Station Road, Delamere, Northwich, Cheshire. CW8 2JQ. Tel: 01606 889941.

 Refreshments: None on route.

Nearest Railway: Cuddington.

290. WHITEHAVEN – ROWRAH, West Cumbria
This is the first section of the Sustrans C2C Route. The trail – dotted with sculptures – climbs slowly away from the industrial Cumbrian Coast towards the western fells of the Lake District.

 The route: Whitehaven harbour – Moor Row – Cleator Moor – Rowrah.

Distance: 9 miles one way, 18 miles both.

Category: Railway path.

Start + Parking: The trail starts by heading south along Preston Street (B5345 towards St Bees). Signposted as the C2C. Several car parks in Whitehaven. Also at Rowrah.

 Surface + Hills: Nearly all tarmac. Gentle climb from Whitehaven to Rowrah.

Roads + Road crossings: Road section at the start in Whitehaven. Otherwise only minor roads to cross.

Links or other nearby trails: Forms part of the C2C Route. Trails around Ennerdale Water and in Whinlatter Forest.

 Map + Leaflet: OS Landranger Map 88. Leaflet available from West Cumbria Groundwork Trust, Crowgarth House, 48 High Street, Cleator Moor, Cumbria. CA25 5AA. Tel: 01946 695678.

 Refreshments: Lots of choice in Whitehaven. Pubs in Cleator Moor and Rowrah.

Nearest Railway: Corkickle Station in the south of Whitehaven.

WILLINGTON COUNTRYWAY,
Bedford – see 210. Priory Country Park and Willington Countryway

291. WILTON OLD ROMAN ROAD,
west of Salisbury
Wilton is a superb base for both both road rides and offroad rides. The lanes tend to follow the valley bottoms (along the Rivers Wylye and Ebble) whereas the offroad rides use the ridges. Most of the offroad rides are only suitable for mountain bikes. This is the easiest of the ridge rides and after a steep climb up from Wilton offers a lovely trip through the beech trees of Grovely Wood.

 The route: Wilton – Grovely Hill – Grovely Wood – Wylye to Dinton road.

Distance: 7 miles one way, 14 miles both.

Category: Old Roman Road.

Start + Parking: Car park in South Street, Wilton. To get to the start, go along West Street (A30 towards Shaftesbury) then turn right by the Bell pub onto Water Ditchampton. Pass beneath a railway bridge then immediately turn left onto a no through road called 'Hollows'. After 1 mile at a 3-way junction of tracks take the right hand one.

 Surface + Hills: Stone/gravel path at the start. Chalk track in parts which may get muddy in winter. One climb of over 350 ft from the start to the highpoint.

Roads + Road crossings: You will need to spend a short time on road in Wilton between the car park and the start of the track.

Links or other nearby trails: Several other rougher bridleways and byways start at Wilton (mountain bikes preferable).

 Map + Leaflet: OS Landranger Map 184.

 Refreshments: Lots of choice in Wilton.

Nearest Railway: Salisbury.

292. WIMBLEDON COMMON,
southwest London
There is a very limited 4 mile network of cycle routes across Wimbledon Common. Signs will indicate where you can and cannot go. The common is a useful link to get to Richmond Park where there is an excellent 8 mile circuit around the park. Leaflet available from Manor Cottage, Wimbledon Common. Tel: 0208 788 7655.

293. WINDSOR GREAT PARK,
west of London
Although there will be occasional vehicles within

Windsor Great Park it is a very cycle-friendly place and an amazing oasis of tranquility set in the heart of such a built-up area. No specific route is described. You are allowed on the tarmac roads (and through the big gates operated by remote control). Signs will tell you where you can't go.

Category: Estate roads through magnificent parkland.

Start + Parking: Bishopsgate Entrance to Windsor Great Park, on the east side of the park, 2 miles south of Old Windsor (off the A328 which links the A30 and the A308).

 Surface + Hills: Tarmac estate roads.

Roads + Road crossings: All on road but there is very little traffic and the visibility is good.

Links or other nearby trails: The **Thames Towpath** and the **Basingstoke Canal** are nearby. Lots of tracks in the Forestry Commission land south of Bracknell (no waymarked trails).

Cycle Hire: Windsor Roller Rink, Alexandra Gardens, tel: 01753 830220.

 Map + Leaflet: OS Landranger Map 175 or maps of the park are available from the ticket office at the Savill Gardens, just south of Bishopgate.

 Refreshments: Pub at Bishopgate. Cafe at Savill Gardens.

Nearest Railway: Windsor.

294. WIRRAL COUNTRY PARK, on the Wirral Peninsula, west of Liverpool
The trail uses a 6 mile section of railway path on the west side of the Wirral Peninsula. There

are plans to extend the path right around the northern edge of the Wirral as far as the ferry terminals that cross the Mersey to Liverpool.

 The route: West Kirby southeast to Heswall.

Distance: 5 miles one way, 10 miles both.

Category: Railway path.

Start + Parking: The Visitor Centre, at the end of the minor road through Thurstaston off the A540 between Heswall and West Kirby.

 Surface + Hills: Stone and gravel path. No hills.

Roads + Road crossings: Short road section in Heswall if you wish to continue to the end of the cycling section of the Wirral Way (at the county boundary with Cheshire, between Gayton and Neston).

Links or other nearby trails: There are plans to continue the trail north around the coastline of the Wirral as far as the Seacombe Ferry. The **Liverpool Loop Line** runs from Halewood to Aintree. There are waymarked trails in **Delamere Forest**. The **Whitegate Way** runs from Cuddington to Winsford.

 Map + Leaflet:
OS Landranger Maps 108 + 117.

 Refreshments: Lots of choice in West Kirby and Heswall.

Nearest Railway: West Kirby.

295. WORCESTER – THE RIVER SEVERN AND THE RACECOURSE
Three short rides starting from the western side of the bridge over the River Severn in Worcester, exploring the banks of the mighty Severn, Worcester Race Course and a section of

the Worcester & Birmingham Canal.

The routes:
1. North from the bridge over the River Severn around the race course.

2. South from the bridge alongside the river.

3. Link to the Worcester & Birmingham Canal at Diglis Basin.

Distance: A total of 6 miles.

Category: Riverside path, canal towpath,

Start + Parking: The long stay car park immediately next to the petrol station, just over the river bridge heading away from Worcester town centre. Follow signs for A44 Leominster over the bridge then imme-diately turn left. From here you can:

1. Cross to the north side of the bridge via the traffic lights, follow the river then cross a pedestrian bridge to do a circuit around the outside of the race course

2. Follow the River Severn south for 1 mile.

3. Cross back over the bridge, walking your bike along the pavement then turn right and follow the riverside path as far as the Diglis Basin. Cross lock and turn left to link with the Worcester & Birmingham Canal Towpath.

Surface + Hills: Fine gravel path.

Roads + Road crossings: The busy A44 is crossed at the west end of the bridge over the River Severn via traffic lights (take care).

Map + Leaflet:
OS Landranger Map 150.

Refreshments: Lots of choice in Worcester.

Nearest Railway: Worcester.

296. WORTH WAY, west of East Grinstead, Sussex
One of two railway paths that start in East Grinstead, the Worth Way whisks you away from commuter land into a wooded landscape in the twinkling of an eye. There is a 0.75 of a mile section along roads through Crawley Down before you dive back into woodland once again.

The route: East Grinstead Railway Station – Crawley Down – Worth (on the eastern edge of Crawley).

Distance: 6.5 miles one way, 13 miles both.

Category: Railway path.

Start + Parking: The car park at the back of the railway station in East Grinstead. Follow the one–way system out of town on the A22 (A264) towards London and Crawley. After passing the railway station on your left, just before a major junction with the A264 Tunbridge Wells road, turn left on to Park Road, then first left on to Grosvenor Road. Turn right into the station car park. The Worth Way starts by a wood-en signpost on the right.

Surface + Hills: Gravel path. No hills.

Roads + Road crossings: Several cross-ings of quiet lanes. Short section through a housing estate in Crawley Down.

Links or other nearby trails: The Forest Way runs southeast from East Grinstead.

Map + Leaflet: OS Landranger Map 187.

Refreshments: Lots of choice in East Grinstead.

Nearest Railway: East Grinstead.

297. YARMOUTH – FRESHWATER, Isle of Wight

This short trail at the western end of the Isle of Wight runs parallel with the atmospheric Yar Estuary between the attractive little port of Yarmouth and the cliffs either side of Freshwater Bay.

 The route: Yarmouth south to Freshwater along the River Yar Estuary.

Distance: 3 miles one way, 6 miles both.

Category: Railway path.

Start + Parking: At the large car park on the southeast edge of Yarmouth. From the car park follow the A3054 towards Newport and Cowes then take the second right onto Mill Road. Follow in the same direction along the estuary of the River Yar.

 Surface + Hills: Stone and gravel path. No hills.

Roads + Road crossings: Short road section at the start and at the southern end if you wish to go into Freshwater Bay.

Links or other nearby trails: The **Cowes to Newport** Trail links the two main towns on the island. There is an excellent ridge ride for mountain bikes along the Tennyson Trail east from Freshwater Bay, up over the golf course, through Brighstone Forest and northeast to Carisbrooke (Newport).

 Map + Leaflet: OS Landranger Map 196.

 Refreshments: Lots of choice in Yarmouth and Freshwater Bay.

Nearest Ferry: Yarmouth.

298. YORK TO BENINGBROUGH

Part of the Sustrans National Cycle Network, the trail starts in the cycle–friendly city of York and follows the course of the River Ouse northwards. The first 5 miles are traffic-free. If you wish to go on to Beningbrough you will need to use quiet lanes for a further 5 miles.

The route:

 Lendal Bridge, York – Esplanade – Clifton Ings – Overton. (Quiet lanes) Overton – Shipton – Beningbrough.

Distance:
5 miles to Overton, 10 miles round trip.
10 miles to Beningbrough, 20 miles round trip.

Category: Riverside path / quiet lanes on National Cycle Network.

Start + Parking:
Lendal Bridge (railway station side) in the centre of York. Any car park near to the railway station. From the south end of Lendal Bridge follow the riverside path westwards 'Acomb, Boroughbridge Road, Chapelfields'. At the second bridge use the steps to cross to the other side of the river to continue following the river northwestwards.

 Surface + Hills: Stone and gravel path. No hills.

Roads + Road crossings: You will need to use quiet lanes for 5 miles if you wish to go to Beningbrough.

Links or other nearby trails: **York to Selby.** There is another railway path in the centre of York (the Foss Island Railpath) which runs eastwards for 3 miles from the Wigginton Road (B1363) near to the hospitals to Osbaldwick.

Cycle Hire:
York Cycle Scene, 2 Radcliffe Street, York.
Tel: 01904 653286.
York Cycle Works, 14–16 Lawrence Street,
York. Tel: 01904 626664.

 Map + Leaflet: OS Landranger
Map 105. York City Council pro-
duces an excellent cycle map for
the city which can be purchased from: The
Cycling Officer, City of York Council,
Environment and Development Services, 9
St Leonard's Place, York. YO1 2ET. Tel: 01904
613161.

 Refreshments: Lots of choice
in York. Tea shop in Beningbrough Hall (closed in winter)

Nearest Railway: York.

299. YORK TO SELBY CYCLE PATH

*Linking the cycle-friendly city of York with the
old town of Selby in the Vale of York across flat,
arable land (and passing the Terry's of York
chocolate factory – breathe in those smells!)*

The route: York –Riccall
– Selby.

Distance: 15 miles one way, 30 miles both.

Category: Railway path.

Start:
Ouse Bridge (railway station side) in the
centre of York at the junction of Skeldergate
and Micklegate. Follow Skeldergate southwards 'Bishopthorpe, Selby' then bear first
left onto Terry Avenue to stay close to the
river and pass beneath Skeldergate Bridge.
This becomes a no through road. Follow the
red tarmac path as it swings away from the

river. Cross the road, cross the race course
and follow signs for Riccall and Selby.

Parking: The route can be picked up from
the Tadcaster Road (Askham Bar) Park and
Ride but bear in mind if an attendant sees
you parking you'll be expected to get on a
bus or risk a £50 fine! The Tesco supermarket next door is possibly a safer bet.

 Surface + Hills: Tarmac. Good
gravel path. No hills.

Roads + Road crossings: Traffic-calmed
roads in York, quiet lanes through Riccall
and into Selby.

Links or other nearby trails: The York
to Beningbrough Route, which forms
part of the National Cycle Network from
Hull to Middlesbrough. There is another
railway path in the centre of York (the Foss
Island Railpath) which runs eastwards for 3
miles from the Wigginton Road (B1363)
near to the hospitals to Osbaldwick.

Cycle Hire:
York Cycle Works, 14-16 Lawrence Street,
York. Tel: 01904 626664.

 Map + Leaflet: OS Landranger
Map 105. York City Council produces an excellent cycle map for
the city which can be purchased
from the City of York Council, Environment
and Development Services, 9 St Leonard's
Place, York. YO1 2ET. Tel: 01904 613161.

 Refreshments: York and Selby.
Two inns and a shop in Riccall.

Nearest Railway: Selby or York.

Long distance routes

There are several sections of the Sustrans' National Cycle Network which are appropriate for cycling holidays of a few days, or a week or two. Listed below are the long-distance routes that are covered by Sustrans award-winning maps.

All the routes involve a mixture of traffic-free paths and quiet lanes.

They are at present all interim routes which means that there are still sections or crossings that need improvement before they meet the high standards required for the fully complete National Cycle Network. These sections are all clearly marked on the route maps.

NATIONAL
cycle network

A MILLENNIUM PROJECT

SUPPORTED BY FUNDS
FROM THE NATIONAL LOTTERY

The Sustrans Official Route Maps and Guides can be purchased from bookshops or from Sustrans Information Service, PO Box 21, Bristol. BS99 2HA. Tel: 0117 929 0888. www.sustrans.org.uk

C2C (Sea to Sea Coast to Coast Route) *140 miles*

Cross the scenic grandeur of Northern England from coast to coast. Savour the delights of the Lake District before a steep ascent to cross the Pennines, followed by a long downhill section to the coast at Newcastle or Sunderland. For those seeking harder challenges there are some tough offroad options. The current map features the link from Penrith to Carlisle, the start of the Scottish National Route.

The Route: Whitehaven (or Workington) - Keswick - Penrith - Allenheads - Consett - Newcastle (or Sunderland). The return C2C is called the Reivers Cycle Route, see below.

Grade: Challenging

DEVON COAST TO COAST. (Plymouth - Ilfracombe) *90 miles*

A southern coast to coast ride! The ride leaves Plymouth along the popular Plym Valley Trail climbing steadily and skirting to the west of the great mass of Dartmoor. The ride crosses the lush green Devon countryside and soon links with the Tarka Trail as it runs north to the coast at Bideford. The railway path loops around the spectacular Taw estuary on its way to the seaside town of Ilfracombe and journey's end. The ride links with the West Country Way.

Grade: Moderate

SCOTTISH NATIONAL ROUTE
From Inverness to Carlisle *400 miles*
Catch a train to Inverness and make your way south through the spectacular Scottish

Highlands to the bonny banks of Loch Lomond. 50 miles of traffic-free paths take you through Glasgow and southwest to the Ayrshire Coast. Cross the great expanse of Galloway Forest Park and finish the ride by following the Solway Firth coastline round to Carlisle.

 Route: Inverness - Newtonmore - Pitlochry - Killin - Callander - Dumbarton - Glasgow - Ayr - Newton Stewart - Dumfries - Carlisle.

Grade: Moderate

LÔN LAS CYMRU.
The Welsh National Route **288 miles**
The toughest section of the National Cycle Network, this spectacular route crosses three mountain ranges and runs the whole length of Wales, from Chepstow or Cardiff to Holyhead. Two routes run north from the Bristol Channel to Builth Wells: the Taff Trail links Cardiff with Brecon via the valleys of South Wales; the Chepstow / Abergavenny option follows quiet lanes through the heart of the Brecon Beacons. The Cambrian Mountains and Snowdonia lie ahead, with challenging offroad options for the brave-hearted.

 Route: Cardiff - Merthyr Tydfil - Brecon - Builth Wells (or Chepstow - Abergavenny - Glasbury - Builth Wells) - Rhayader - Llanidloes - Machynlleth - Criccieth - Caernarfon - Bangor - Holyhead.

Grade: Very challenging

HULL TO HARWICH **369 miles**
The easiest section of the National Cycle Network, the Hull to Harwich route crosses the gentle countryside of Eastern England from the Lincolnshire Wolds and Fens and runs down into Norfolk and Suffolk. After the Wolds the route rarely rises above 200 ft making it ideal for families or adults returning to cycling. Linking

the ports of Hull and Harwich the route explores the cathedral cities of Lincoln and Norwich and visits many attractive East Anglian villages on its way through Constable country.

 Route: Hull - Beelsby - Market Rasen - Lincoln - Boston - Wisbech - Kings Lynn - Burnham Market - Fakenham - Norwich - Beccles - Peasenhall - Ipswich - Colchester - Harwich.

Grade: Easy

KINGFISHER TRAIL
An Irish Figure of Eight **220 miles**
Explore the Emerald Isle on the Kingfisher Trail. The 220 mile route is in the form of a figure of eight which crosses and recrosses the border between the Republic of Ireland and Northern Ireland, taking in the scenic Upper and Lower Lough Erne and the beautiful hills of Leitrim. Enjoy the warmth and friendliness of the locals and get a taste for Guinness in its home country. Catch a ferry from Stranraer or Liverpool to Belfast or from Holyhead to Dublin.

Grade: Moderate

WHITE ROSE CYCLE ROUTE FROM HULL TO MIDDLESBROUGH **140 miles**
With its gentle gradients, the White Rose Cycle Route links the river systems of the Humber and the Tees via the Yorkshire Wolds, the historic city of York and the Vale of York. From Hull there are two options: one runs parallel with the Humber and Ouse to Selby, the other heads north before crossing rolling wold country. They link in York, one of Britain's most cycle-friendly cities. An optional side trip explores the steep challenges of the spectacular Yorkshire Moors. The southern end includes a link with the Harwich to Hull route.

Grade: Easy

CLYDE TO THE FORTH
(Glasgow - Edinburgh) *86 miles*
Cycle across Scotland at its narrowest point from the Firth of Clyde to the Firth of Forth using a mixture of roads, railway paths and canal towpaths. The ride starts at Gourock with its ferry terminal to Dunoon on the spectacular Cowal Peninsula. Savour the panoramic views across the water to the hills behind Helensburgh. Turning inland to Johnstone, the ride passes through Glasgow and out to the Airdrie-Bathgate railway path before linking with the Union Canal into the heart of Edinburgh with its wealth of magnificent architecture.

Grade: Easy

SEVERN TO THE THAMES (Severn Bridge - Newbury) *100 miles*
Linking two of the country's major rivers, this gentle ride across southern England runs from the old Severn Bridge to the Thames at Reading. After the historic city of Bristol, follow the railway path into Bath with its beautiful honey-coloured stone buildings. Breeze along the towpath of the scenic Kennet and Avon Canal over spectacular viaducts and past an amazing flight of locks. From Devizes the route diverts onto quiet lanes to Newbury. A northern alternative passes through the fine old towns of Chippenham and Marlborough before rejoining the main route.

Grade: Easy

WEST COUNTRY WAY
From Padstow to Bristol *250 miles*
The West Country Way is a celebration of all the best cycling in this part of the world, linking the Cornish Coast at Padstow to the historic cities of Bath and Bristol via the highly popular traffic-free Camel and Tarka Trails. It takes in an exhilarating ridge ride over the roof of Exmoor and includes two lovely sections of canal towpath. The atmospheric Somerset Levels, the mystical town of Glastonbury and the glory of Wells Cathedral are all highlights of the final third of the ride with an easy finish along the Bristol & Bath railway path.

The Route: Padstow – Bodmin – Bude – Barnstaple – Tiverton – Taunton – Bridgwater – Wells – (Bath) – Bristol.

Grade: Moderate/challenging

THE REIVERS CYCLE ROUTE – The Return C2C, Northumberland - Cumbria *180 miles*
Cycling A to B is fine for some but many cycle tourists want their rides to be A to A. To cater for this demand, and to spread the economic benefits of the C2C (Sea to Sea) northwards into the borders, a consortium of local authorities, tourist boards and the recreation wings of Forest Enterprise and Northumbrian Water have devised the Reivers Route, a 180-mile Return C2C

The Reivers Route goes north from the C2C on Tyneside, crosses Hadrian's Wall country and runs parallel to the Roman ruins for much of its length. The central point is Kielder Water, Europe's largest man-made lake. This area was the Wild West of the 15th and 16th centuries, a lawless buffer zone between Scotland and England, peopled by lawless Lords, cattle rustlers, ruffians, ne'er-do-wells and bandits, known collectively as Reivers. Because of these past troubles the Reivers Route passes many imposing castles and fortified farmhouses.

The Reivers Way – route number 10 on the National Cycle Network – opened in May 1998. It's easier than the C2C but, in parts, much more remote so B&Bs are often few and far between. Ditto for pubs, shops and cafes. Plan ahead!

Grade: Moderate

THAMES VALLEY CYCLE ROUTE (LONDON - OXFORD)

Starting at Putney Bridge, escape from London through Richmond Park and along the banks of the majestic River Thames passing Hampton Court and Runnymede. After the vast splendour of Windsor Castle the route travels cross-country to rejoin the river at Wargrave, then threads its way through Reading. Glorious Chiltern beech-woods form a canopy over the lanes as you climb north past the Maharajah's Well at Stoke Row to historic Wallingford and Abingdon before reaching journey's end among the dreaming spires of Oxford.

Grade: Easy

YORK TO NOTTINGHAM CYCLE ROUTE

Travel down the Vale of York from Britain's most cycle-friendly city, wave at the racehorses at Doncaster's St Leger, buy some cutlery in Sheffield before crossing the great estates of the Dukeries. Robin Hood's Merry Men will guide you across Sherwood Forest and D.H. Lawrence country into the heart of Nottingham.

Grade: Moderate

THE CELTIC TRAIL (WEST) (FISHGUARD TO SWANSEA)

The route explores the beautiful Pembrokeshire coastline as far as St David's before turning SE towards Pembroke Castle and Laugharne, home of Dylan Thomas. Beyond Carmarthen the route enters the Llanelli Millennium Coastal Park and finishes along the wide sweep of Swansea Bay.

Grade: Moderate (with challenging options)

THE CELTIC TRAIL (EAST) (SWANSEA - SEVERN BRIDGE)

South Wales was once the world's greatest coal-producing area and though the pits have gone, there are still many signs of the area's rich industrial heritage in the form of old railways, viaducts and canals, many of which are used on this route through the Welsh Valleys to the old Severn Bridge at Chepstow.

Grade: Moderate (with challenging options)

EDINBURGH TO ABERDEEN CYCLE ROUTE

From the beautiful city of Edinburgh the route crosses the famous Forth Road Bridge into the Kingdom of Fife and the historic town of St Andrews before continuing north along the coast via Dundee and smoky ol' Arbroath up to the granite city of Aberdeen.

Grade: Moderate

ABERDEEN TO INVERNESS CYCLE ROUTE (INCLUDES EXTENSION TO WICK AND THURSO)

North of Aberdeen the route passes through the red-sandstone town of Turriff before reaching the Moray Firth at the fishing port of Banff. West from here you pass through the attractive settlements at Portsoy, Forres and Nairn. Beyond Inverness, 'capital' of the Highlands, there are options to continue north to Thurso or Wick.

Grade: Moderate

EAST MIDLANDS CYCLE ROUTE (OXFORD TO DERBY)

Highlights along this route through the geographical centre of England include the the old town of Winslow and the amazing cycle network in Milton Keynes. Traffic-free sections include the Brampton Valley Way between Northampton and Market Harborough, a river-side path through Leicester and the finish along the River Derwent into Derby.

Grade: Moderate

TRAIL the UK's number one adventure walking and outdoors lifestyle magazine

THE MOST AUTHORITATIVE GEAR TESTS AVAILABLE

AWE-INSPIRING PHOTOGRAPHY, BRILLIANT READS

STUNNING WALKING, BIKING AND CLIMBING ROUTES

On sale now from all good newsagents

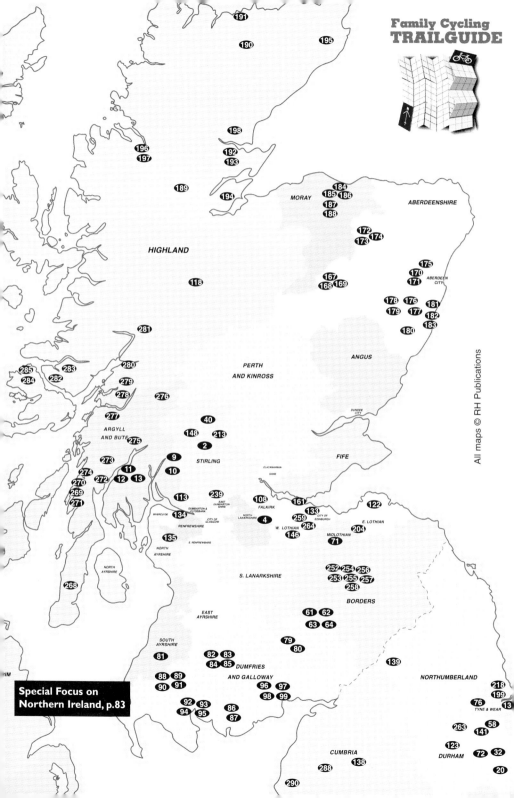

All maps © RH Publications

191

190

195

198

196
197

192
193

189

194

MORAY

184
185 186
187
188

ABERDEENSHIRE

172
173 174

HIGHLAND

118

175
170
171   ABERDEEN CITY

167
168 169

178 176
179 177
180

181
182
183

281

280

ANGUS

PERTH AND KINROSS

DUNDEE CITY

285
284

283

282

279

278

276

40

148   213

2

281

273

277

ARGYLL AND BUTE
275

9

STIRLING

FIFE

10

274
270
269
271

272

11
12   13

CLACKMANNAN-
SHIRE

113

239

108

161

133

122

DUMBARTON & CLYDEBANK

EAST DUNBARTON-
SHIRE

FALKIRK

259
CITY OF
EDINBURGH

WHERCLYDE

134

CITY OF GLASGOW

NORTH LANARKSHIRE

4

264

E. LOTHIAN

204

RENFREWSHIRE

146

MIDLOTHIAN

71

135

E. RENFREWSHIRE

W. LOTHIAN

NORTH AYRSHIRE

S. LANARKSHIRE

252 254 256
253 255 257
258

NORTH AYRSHIRE

BORDERS

268

EAST AYRSHIRE

61 62
63 64

79

80

SOUTH AYRSHIRE

81

139

82 83
84 85   DUMFRIES

NORTHUMBERLAND

218
199
13

88 89
90 91

AND GALLOWAY

96 97
98 99

76
TYNE & WEAR

**Special Focus on
Northern Ireland, p.83**

92 93
94 95

86
87

263

58
141

123

DURHAM

72 32

CUMBRIA

288   138

20

290

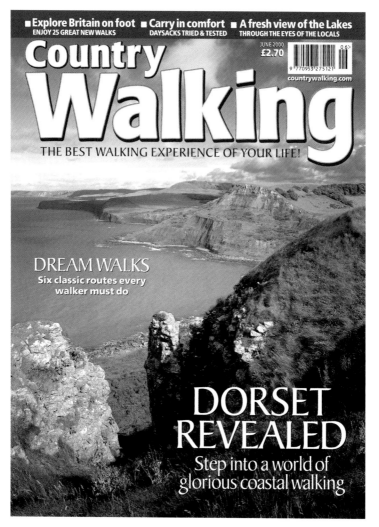

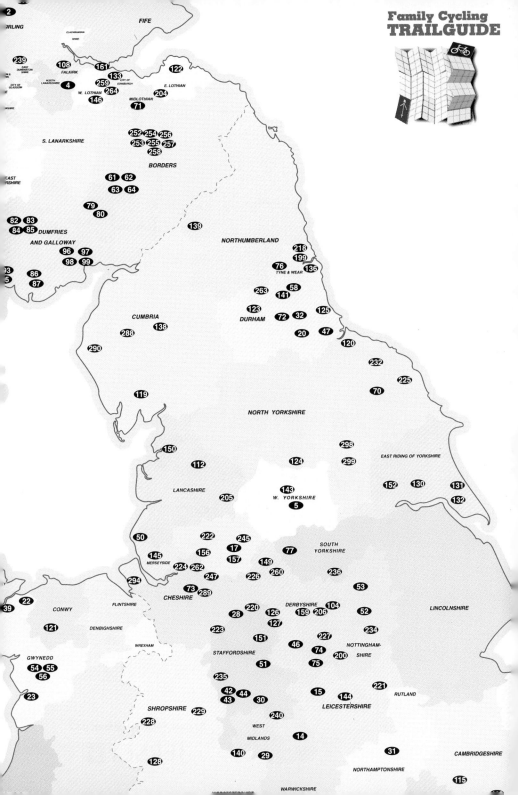

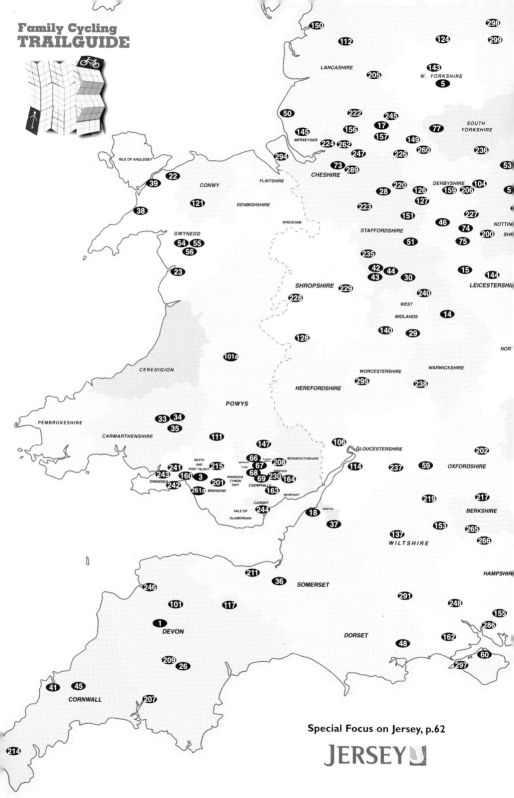

Family Cycling TRAILGUIDE

150
112
298
124
299
LANCASHIRE
143
205
W. YORKSHIRE
5
50
222
245
145
156
17
77
SOUTH
YORKSHIRE
MERSEYSIDE
224
262
157
149
294
247
226
260
236
73
289
CHESHIRE
53
ISLE OF ANGLESEY
22
220
104
39
CONWY
FLINTSHIRE
28
126
159
206
5
38
121
DENBIGHSHIRE
223
127
WREXHAM
151
227
NOTTIN
GWYNEDD
STAFFORDSHIRE
46
74
200
SHI
54
55
51
75
56
235
15
23
42
44
144
43
30
LEICESTERSHIRE
SHROPSHIRE
229
240
228
WEST
MIDLANDS
14
CEREDIGION
128
140
29
NOR
101a
WORCESTERSHIRE
WARWICKSHIRE
POWYS
295
238
HEREFORDSHIRE
PEMBROKESHIRE
33
34
147
106
GLOUCESTERSHIRE
202
35
111
66
208
CARMARTHENSHIRE
NEATH
67
MONMOUTHSHIRE
237
59
OXFORDSHIRE
241
215
MERTHYR
TYDFIL
68
114
243
160
3
69
230
BLAENAU
GWENT
SWANSEA
201
RHONDDA
CYNON
TAFF
164
219
217
242
261a
BRIDGEND
163
CAERPHILLY
BERKSHIRE
NEWPORT
265
CARDIFF
244
137
153
18
266
VALE OF
GLAMORGAN
BRISTOL
37
WILTSHIRE
HAMPSHIR
211
36
SOMERSET
291
248
246
155
101
117
286
1
DEVON
48
DORSET
60
209
26
297
41
45
207
CORNWALL
214

Special Focus on Jersey, p.62

JERSEY

THE WATERWAYS CODE:
Cycling on the towpath

This is the Towpath Safety Code from British Waterways.

1. Give way to other people on the towpath and warn them politely of your approach. A 'hello' and a 'thank you' mean a lot.

2. Access paths can be steep and slippery – join the towpath with care.

3. Dismount if the towpath is busy with walkers or anglers.

4. Get off and push your cycle – if the path gets very narrow when passing beneath low bridges and alongside locks or if you encounter any other danger

5. Ride at a gentle pace, in single file and do not bunch. Never race – remember you have water on one side of you.

6. If you are a young or inexperienced cyclist, always go with a responsible adult.

7. Watch out for hidden mooring spikes or ropes across the path beside moored boats.

8. Take particular care on wet or uneven surfaces and don't worsen them by skidding.

9. Never cycle along the towpath in the dark.

10. You are responsible for your own and others' safety.

11. Your bike should have a bell or hooter.

12. Spiky hedge trimmings can cause a puncture. We do our best to tidy them up, but recommend plastic tyre inserts just in case.

For any enquiries, including the latest situation on permits, contact:

Customer Services
British Waterways,
Willow Grange,
Chuch Road,
Watford.
WD1 3QA.

Tel: 01923 201120

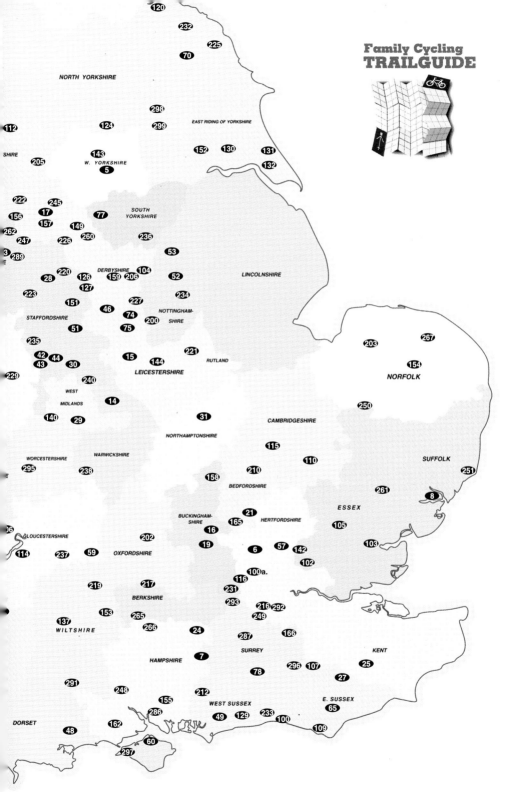

**Family Cycling
TRAILGUIDE**

Got a bike?

Then make it work for you – advice on how to improve your fitness > Need somewhere to ride? Check out our events section > Need inspiration? Our destinations section is on hand to get you in the saddle > Plus adventure racing and details of adventure camps > Oh, and everything you could possibly want to know about running.

GET DIRTY
Running fitness magazine. On sale every 4 weeks

NOTES